DRAGO DESCENDING

ALSO BY GREG F. GIFUNE

Novels

A View from the Lake
A Winter Sleep
Babylon Terminal
Blood in Electric Blue
Children of Chaos
Deep Night
Devil's Breath
Dominion
Gardens of Night
Judas Goat
Long After Dark
Midnight Solitaire
Night Work
Orphans of Wonderland
Rogue
Savages
Saying Uncle
The Bleeding Season
The Living and the Dead
Dangerous Boys

Novellas

Apartment Seven
Catching Hell
Drago Descending
Dreams the Ragman
House of Rain
Kingdom of Shadows
Lords of Twilight
Oasis of the Damned
Sorcerer
The Rain Dancers
Midnight Gods

Collections

Down to Sleep
Beneath the Night
Heretics

GREG F. GIFUNE

DRAGO DESCENDING

Author's Preferred Edition

DRAGO DESCENDING

An Introduction

In 1999, I was still a struggling writer with dreams of being a professional novelist. I'd had some short stories and articles published in magazines and anthologies all over the world, and as I was even getting paid in actual cash now and then, I'd managed to at least approach becoming a professional at that. I'd only written one novel at that point, a crime thriller called *Night Work* I wrote in 1996, which would eventually go on to be published, but hadn't yet sold. Beyond that, I'd only written short fiction and nonfiction articles. Back then the internet had been available to the general public for about a decade, but it was a lot different than it is now in 2018, and writers still used a lot of trade magazines and publications for leads on publishers looking for submissions. After consulting one of my regular trades, I saw that a small but reputable professional publisher was looking for novellas. They planned to publish across several genres, had a nice distribution deal with booksellers nationally and online, and were open to unsolicited submissions (in-other-words, you didn't need a literary agent in order to submit your work, and since I didn't have an agent at the time that was a big deal because not a lot of publishers worked that way back then). After checking the cutoff time for submissions, I decided I'd have just enough time to sit down and write the short novel I'd been thinking about for a couple years. I worked day and night for three months, until the first draft was finished. It wasn't ready to go out into the world, though, so I put it through several edits, did numerous rewrites then sent it to a couple mentors I was fortunate enough to have at the time. They read it, made some great suggestions which I implemented, and then I edited it once more. Four months after starting it, I had what I considered to be a completed novella ready to be submitted.

Drago Descending was born.

By the time I sent the novella in, 1999 had become 2000. After several weeks of waiting, I received an answer in the form of a large manila envelope in my PO Box. I was more accustomed to finding stacks of business envelopes in there, since back then, that's how most rejections came. I remember sitting in my car with that manila envelope in my lap and just staring at it. When I finally found the courage to rip it open, an acceptance letter and contract fell out. They loved *Drago Descending* and wanted to publish it in paperback. They even offered me a generous advance. The figure was more than all of the paychecks I'd received as a writer to that point combined. To say I was pleased would be an understatement. I was on my way. Finally!

Except, I really wasn't, because a month later, before my advance check arrived and while *Drago Descending* was still sitting in the que to be published, the company folded. My chance had come and gone, and I was right back where I'd started.

I drank a lot of vodka that week.

It would go on to be accepted by another company that also unexpectedly went out of business before it could be published, and I began to think maybe the whole thing was cursed and destined to remain in my desk drawer forever. As it turned out, it took two more years, but eventually, *Drago Descending* found a home with a small publisher in 2002. When it was all said and done, it did fairly well commercially, stayed in print for a few years, got good reviews and positive reaction from readers, and helped launch my career as a novelist. But it never made quite the splash I'd hoped for, so when the contract ended, I opted not to renew with that publisher and let *Drago Descending* go out of print.

For several years it remained unavailable, and the only place you might be able to find one was as a used copy on the secondary market. I left it out of print purposely, but not because I didn't want it out there, I did, I just didn't feel like I'd found the right publisher for it. Actually, I wasn't sure such a publisher even existed or ever would again. Suffice to say, an occult hardboiled noir private detective thriller isn't exactly an easy market, and as my career as a novelist took off, I was occupied with other projects and decided to pursue new works rather than attempt to get *Drago Descending* back into print. So it sat, largely forgotten, except by its hardcore fans. In the time it was in print, *Drago Descending* garnered a small but fiercely enthusiastic following that absolutely loved it. Many hoped it might be the start of a series, and some sent fan letters with new adventures they'd love to see David Drago tackle. Some sent me fan fiction versions of their ideas, and one reader even produced the only hardcover edition of *Drago Descending* in existence, producing only three copies, one for himself, one for me, and one for the publisher, all at his own expense and without my knowledge until it arrived in the mail for me. Not entirely legal at the time due to copyright issues, of course, but since none were ever to be sold, I saw no reason it would become an issue (and it never did). Still, it was a gesture that moved me deeply, one I'll never forget, and a testament to just how beloved by some *Drago Descending* was and continues to be.

Thankfully, I went to work with the fine folks at Down & Out Books a couple years ago (publishers of my novels *Dangerous Boys*, *Saying Uncle* and *Night Work*), and when Eric Campbell asked if I had any out-of-print works from my backlist that might work for them, I immediately thought of *Drago Descending*. I gave him a brief synopsis, he loved the concept, and accepted it sight unseen.

So now, as I write this in 2018, I've just finished the *Author's Preferred Edition* of *Drago Descending* for its new publisher, and while it's essentially the same story, it has been tweaked a bit with a few minor changes I'd wanted originally (but didn't have the juice to demand back then). It's a vastly different world than when *Drago Descending* was first written and published, and since the novella is largely set in 1999, you'll notice not everyone has cell phones, there are still such things as payphones, VCRs and videocassettes, and people still smoke in restaurants and in various public and social situations. Hopefully that all seems more oddly charming than dated these days, as it fits the time in which it was written and remains loyal to the original piece, which I felt was important not only to the loyal fans of this novella who have continued to love it for all these years, but to those new readers who are about to discover *Drago Descening* for the very first time.

I'm in a very different place now professionally and personally than I was in 1999 (something for which I will always be grateful), and this time around *Drago Descending* is getting the treatment and release I'd always hoped for. I could not be happier to send it back out into the world once again, and between you and me, I'm just as excited to see *Drago Descending* find a new home and a host of new readers as I was that day I sat in my junky old car, nervously staring at that manila envelope and hoping for the best.

Here's to David Drago, wherever he is these days.

This is his story.

Greg F. Gifune
2018
New England
Night

v

For Carol

*And in loving memory of the
one and only Justin Quinn*

*"Acts of injustice done
Between the setting and the rising sun
In history lie like bones, each one."*
—W.H. Auden, The Ascent of F.6

1991

Chapter 1

Dawn had been approaching for hours. Soft shades of gray punctured holes in an otherwise black sky; the light emerging on the horizon like the slow and steady drip of blood from a fresh wound. The night was seamless— with no beginning, no end—and reality had become strangely malleable.

Just miles from Baghdad, I nestled deeper into my cradle of rock below a large ridge, felt desert sand sift between my legs and remembered the roar of the aircraft as it plummeted to Earth. The others didn't survive, and I'd been alone from that point forward.

Ignoring the blood on my chest, stomach and hands, I climbed to the edge of the ridge, and through night-vision goggles, focused on an encampment of ten enemy soldiers.

I returned to my hiding place and clutched my rifle like a child awakened from nightmares. As my thoughts turned to Jesse and the world I'd known before, I began to understand why I could never leave this hellish place alive...

1999

Chapter 2

Rain clicked against the windows like acrylic fingernails tapping a computer keyboard. I pushed the memories of that ancient desert aside, spun around in my desk chair and watched the blurred view of the street just outside my office. Despite the beautiful foliage, October in New England was raw and gloomy enough; the rain only made it worse.

I opened the morning edition of the *Times* and spread it out across my desk. Little had changed in New Bedford in the last twenty-four hours. There had been a shooting in the south end of the city just blocks from my office, the mayoral primaries were getting nastier by the minute, and the forecast predicted continued showers and heavy winds for most of Southeastern Massachusetts.

I was just about to start a crossword puzzle when the phone rang. "Drago Investigations."

"Is Mr. Drago in?" a soft male voice asked.

"That'd be me."

"Would it be possible to make an appointment?"

"Depends. What can I do for you?"

"I need the services of a professional investigator," he said evenly. "That *is* what you do, isn't it?"

I glanced at the layer of dust covering my appointment book. "Theoretically." Silence—no sense of humor, this guy. "What sort of work you need done?"

"I'd prefer to discuss this in person, if you don't mind."

"Did you have a particular time in mind?"

"My schedule is relatively flexible."

I ruffled some papers to make it sound good. "I could squeeze you in today if you can make it around ten o'clock."

"That's fine," the man answered. "I assume the address in the phone book is still current?"

"Yeah, it…it is…" I looked over at the cot I'd set up in the corner and the array of spent beer and liquor bottles, empty pizza boxes and dirty laundry scattered across the floor and along the top of my file cabinets. Due to a decided lack of business, I'd been forced to give up my apartment and live out of the office for the past few weeks. "But my office is undergoing a bit of renovation at the moment. Tell me, Mr.—"

"Abdiel."

"Say again?"

"A-B-D-I-E-L. Abdiel."

"Uh-huh. Are you familiar with New Bedford, sir?"

"I am."

"Meet me at the Moby City Cafe. It's across from the bus station downtown."

"Perfect. I'll see you at ten o'clock."

I hung up and thumbed through the stack of bills on the corner of my desk. "Thank God."

Chapter 3

The drive to the bus terminal took less than five minutes. I parked on the street, flipped up the collar on my leather jacket and sprinted through the rain to the cafe.

Once inside I was greeted by a comforting burst of heat and a heavyset hostess positioned behind a cash register. "Morning, Dave." She smiled. "Nice weather, huh?"

I shook excess water from my hands and glanced first at the stools along the counter and then at a sea of small tables near the back. A cross section of senior citizens and working stiffs occupied most of the space, but none of them seemed to notice me. "You lose some weight, Anna?"

"Oh, definitely," she said, chuckling. "I'm wasting away to nothing."

"Well, you look even more fabulous than usual."

"You always say that."

"And I always mean it."

"Your game could use some originality, but I give you points for effort."

"I'm meeting a client," I explained. "Can I get a table in back?"

Anna grabbed a laminated menu from behind the counter and offered it to me. "He's already here, hon. Asked for you when he came in. I sat him in the corner over by the kitchen."

"Thanks. Just a coffee when you get a chance, okay?"

As I approached our table, I saw a tall, sinewy man of perhaps forty sitting casually in a chair facing the entrance. Dressed in a pair of expensive slacks, Italian loafers and a heavy wool sweater that probably cost more than everything I had on put together, Mr. Abdiel was not what I'd expected. He rose slowly to his feet, extended a hand and smiled at me with a set of perfect, bright teeth. "Mr. Drago?"

His grip was firm, warm, but not aggressive. "Yeah, hi, I—sorry to be so abrupt on the phone," I said, "but I get a lot of telemarketing calls pretending to be potential clients."

"Don't give it another thought." He waited to return to his seat until I had taken mine. "I appreciate you seeing me on such short notice. I'm sure you're very busy."

I lit a cigarette, responded with a smile and studied his features. His mane of hair caught my attention first. A medium shade of brown, it was parted in the middle and tumbled in large silky curls nearly to his shoulders. It reminded me of the wigs the Three Musketeers wore in the old comic strips, only not quite that long. Obviously, it was a ridiculous hairstyle for anyone—particularly a man his age—but he somehow managed to pull it off. His blue eyes were small and deep-seated, his nose long, straight, and his chin pronounced. His complexion was clear and well cared for, and his hands bore none of the scars of one who labored for a living. I noticed an ankle-length cashmere coat draped over the back of his chair and tried not to stare. "So what's on your mind, Mr. Abdiel? What can I do for you?"

He slid his chair away from the edge of the table so he could comfortably cross his legs. "I understand a good deal of what you do involves missing persons, yes?"

"Did someone recommend me?" I asked.

"Not exactly, no."

"I used to do a lot of fraud cases, but the insurance companies prefer to use larger investigation firms these days. Mostly what I do now involves background checks and domestic concerns, but I've handled my share of missing-persons jobs. Teenage runaways or people who go to the corner store for a gallon of milk and keep right on going, that sort of thing."

"Do you mind if I ask what your rate of success is?"

"Everything's computerized these days," I told him. "It makes things a lot easier than they used to be in terms of tracking folks down, because it's harder to disappear. There's still legwork involved, but I usually don't have too many problems. Of course it depends on the situation, the person and other factors. Every case is different."

"I see." Abdiel's eyes blinked slowly, like a cat's. "Could you give me a brief overview of your background?"

"I've been in private investigations for a little over five years now. Before that, I did a stint in the military, and prior to that I was a police officer here in the city."

"Is this where you're from originally?"

I took a long pull on my cigarette. "Yeah. You?"

"I live in Plymouth at the moment," he said with an air of caution, "but I'm originally from up north."

"Maine?"

Abdiel smiled. "Further north."

"A Canadian, huh?"

Before he could answer, Anna appeared with my coffee, set it on the table and moved away without comment. I left my cigarette between my lips and warmed my hands along the sides of the mug. "Let's cut to the chase. Who do you need found?"

Abdiel gave a lengthy sigh. "I'm going to be completely honest with you, Mr. Drago. You and I have a common friend."

Confusion set in since I was relatively certain I didn't have any friends. "And who would that be?"

His pale blue eyes met mine. "Jesse Greenlaw."

A wide range of emotion surged through me—too many to focus on one specifically—and I made no attempt to mask my expression. "What do you want?"

Abdiel blushed and nervously fingered a napkin. "I was afraid the mention of her name might make you angry," he said softly, "but I assure you it's not my intention to give you a hard time. Jesse disappeared nearly a month ago."

"She did the same thing to me, chief."

He leaned forward, placing his forearms on the table between us. "You don't understand. Jesse and I are engaged to be married. She'd been living with me in Plymouth for the past two years. I met her about a year after the two of you split up."

"I didn't realize she was back in the area," I said. "And we didn't split up. She left me."

Abdiel gave a short, rapid nod. "Jesse spoke of you often, Mr. Drago. She described you as her first true love. She said you two were together a long time."

"We met in high school," I heard myself say.

"Jesse told me that after you returned from the Gulf

War the two of you lived together for more than a year," he said. "Generally she spoke of that time fondly, but she also said it eventually became painfully apparent that you'd grown apart."

I grabbed my cigarette, took an angry drag and exhaled through my nose. "Not that it's any of your business, but I wanted more of a traditional lifestyle. The house, the dog, the kids—you know the routine—but she was still dreaming about Hollywood. When I came home, I found out she'd taken a job stripping at a club over in Brockton. She was banking money so we could move to Los Angeles. Only problem was, that wasn't what I was looking for."

A police car rushed past the cafe, siren blaring, but Abdiel didn't seem to notice. "I'm an only child. My father was very successful, and when he passed on he left me a considerable amount of money."

"Congratulations."

"The point is, I've spent most of my adult life moving from one business venture to another," Abdiel continued. "I met some people a few years back and had an opportunity to invest in a film project being produced in New York. That's where I first met Jesse. At the time she was enjoying a very successful film career."

"Meryl Streep has a film career," I said. "Jesse made porno flicks."

Abdiel glanced around uncomfortably and struggled to clear his throat. "Yes, well…at any rate…I was investing in the film she was making and that's how we met. We started dating not long after and things eventually became serious between us. We moved in together and, as I say, had planned to be married. She had a few contractual agreements she had to fulfill but was planning to leave the business once they'd been completed. Things were difficult for a while because most of her gigs were in New York, but her final project was filmed on Cape Cod. On the final day of shooting, she left the location and told everyone she was headed home. She never arrived."

"You haven't seen or heard from her since?" I asked.

Abdiel shook his head in the negative. "It's as if she vanished into thin air."

"So go to the cops and file a missing person report."

"I'd rather not involve the police in this."

I sipped some coffee and tossed a dollar bill on the table. "It's been more than five years since I've seen Jesse Greenlaw, and I'm still trying to forget I ever met her. The last thing in the world I want to do is try to find her."

"Wait," he said, leaning closer. "What is the fee you normally charge?"

"Seventy-five bucks an hour, plus expenses, but—"

"—I'll double it."

I pushed my chair back and stood up. "Not interested, but I can recommend a couple agencies that—"

"No," he interrupted, "it's you I want. You know Jesse, you know her habits, and despite what you've said I'm sure you still care about what happens to her. I know I can count on you to do everything in your power to find her. I'll pay you two hundred dollars an hour, plus any expenses."

I wanted to leave, but my feet refused to cooperate. With a sigh, I sank back down into the chair. "Are you out of your mind?"

"I love her."

"You can do a lot better than me for that kind of coin."

Abdiel seemed to relax to the extent that he was capable. "I'm also prepared to give you an advance of three thousand dollars. In cash, of course."

I damn near wet my pants. The three grand alone was enough to dig me out of debt for a month or two. "Look, what if she doesn't want to come back? Even if I find her it's not like I'm a cop, I can't interfere—legally, I'm talking—I can't force her to—"

"I only want to know where she is," he insisted, "and that she's all right."

"I can't make any promises."

"I'm not asking you to." He reached behind him, removed an envelope from his coat and placed it on the table. "Feel free to count it if you'd like."

I did. Three thousand bucks later the envelope exchanged places with a small notepad in my inside jacket pocket. "The last time you saw her was the final day of shooting?"

Abdiel crossed his legs and resumed a more informal pose. "Yes, the morning of her final day on the Cape Cod project."

"Anything strange about her behavior?"

"Nothing that I remember."

"Any arguments or anything along those lines? Deep talks?"

"No."

I looked up from my pad. "Obviously you had an open relationship. Was she seeing anyone else at the time?"

He nibbled his lower lip as if to prevent a smile. "Jesse only had relations with the people she worked with on film, Mr. Drago. In the real world, we were monogamous."

"You sure about that?"

"Yes."

I pretended to write something down while I thought of the next question. "Did she take anything with her when she left that day?"

"The clothes on her back, her purse and her car."

"What sort of car?"

"A 1998 Mercedes sports coupe. Bronze, registered to her."

She'd driven a battered Ford Escort when I'd known her, but I didn't see any point in mentioning that. "Has she touched any of her bank accounts since she left?"

"We'd already opened joint accounts in anticipation of our marriage," Abdiel explained. "She's made no withdrawals."

"Was she carrying any credit cards?"

"Visa and an American Express Gold."

"Any activity on either account?"

"None."

I took a quick sip of coffee and signaled Anna for a refill, but she didn't see me. "When I knew Jesse, she played around with drugs from time to time. Was she still using?"

"I know she smoked pot to relax now and then, and she often did a bit of cocaine when she was working—most of the women do—but other than that, no."

"She still drink?"

Abdiel nodded. "Socially."

"She was pretty goddamn sociable when I knew her, so does *socially* still mean a lot?"

"Jesse drank a tad more than she should have, yes."

"Was she on any medication?"

"None that I'm aware of."

I waited a while before asking the next one. "Jesse was always a bit of a wild-child, but did she have any breakdowns or episodes or exhibit any signs of mental illness or emotional distress?"

"Just the opposite," he said. "She was always in control, always so strong and confident in herself. It's one of the things I found most attractive about her, actually."

"Uh-huh. She got any enemies you know of?"

"Jesse worked in a very cutthroat business. Certainly there were people she didn't always get along with, but I can't think of anyone who'd want to do her bodily harm."

"I'll need the name and either an address or phone number, email—something—of the people she was working for on that last film," I said. "They won't know I got the information from you; I'll keep your name out of it."

Abdiel gave me the name and office address of the film producer, Walter Rizzi, located in Hyannis. "I'll also need the names of any close friends."

"Jesse was a loner, as you know. Except for me she really wasn't close to anyone. There were several acquaintances, both professional and personal, but no one I'd describe as a friend per se."

"Do you have a recent photo?"

He produced one from his wallet, glanced at it briefly and handed it over. My heart began to race and a cool sweat broke out across my palms, the same as when I'd first laid eyes on her. She'd bleached her hair and it was longer, fuller than I remembered, but there was no disguising the mischievous glint in those emerald eyes. Clad in a skimpy bikini and stretched out on a chaise lounge, she looked as if she hadn't aged a day since the last time

I'd seen her.

"That was taken just last summer," Abdiel said.

I returned the photograph and notepad to my jacket pocket. "How do I get in touch with you?"

"As I'm sure you can imagine," he said in a quiet, conspiratorial tone, "I have other business interests, so discretion is of the utmost important. I'd be more comfortable contacting you."

"Fine." I handed him one of my business cards. "The first number will put you through to my office. The second is my pager. Today's Friday. Give me a call first thing Monday morning and we'll see where we stand at that point. I'll be discrete as possible, but at some point if this involves anything beyond any a basic looksee, I'll need some contact info."

"I understand."

"Good. Anything else I need to know?"

Without looking at me, Abdiel said, "They say love is the greatest gift God ever bestowed on us, yet at times loving someone so desperately feels more like a curse."

"True enough."

"It must have been difficult to lose her after all you'd been through. You know, with the war and all."

My response was not immediate. "Ever been in combat, Mr. Abdiel?"

"As a matter of fact, I have." He collected his features into a polite smile. "But I don't like to discuss it."

"That makes two of us."

"Jesse was very proud of your service," he said. "She often referred to you as a war hero."

I took a final drag on my cigarette before grinding it out in the ashtray. "There's no such thing."

Chapter 4

My elderly Chevy Nova stalled twice on the way back to the office. If that wasn't enough, someone had taken my parking space, forcing me to find a spot on the next block. By the time I'd reached the entrance to my building, I was soaked to the bone.

After toweling off and changing into a fresh shirt, I turned on my computer and tapped into an outlaw people finder program I often used that located by name, address and phone number everyone in the United States with a social security number. I entered Jesse's full name, consulted my notes, then keyed in the last known address in Plymouth Abdiel had given me.

While waiting for the program to run through the motions, I leaned back in my desk chair and tried to relax. It had taken me more than five years to reach the point where a single day might pass without Jesse's memory haunting me, and now all the pain, anger and confusion had resurfaced in one frantic rush. I felt like an alcoholic who had been pushed off the wagon while his back was turned, and I had little doubt that the deeper my involvement became in this case, the worse things were likely to get.

There was only one Jessica Greenlaw listed in Plymouth and the address matched the one I'd entered. The phone number came up unlisted, and since there was nothing to indicate that the information already in my possession was anything but current, I entered her name again, this time requesting a search of the entire state of Massachusetts. A list of six Greenlaws appeared but only one Jessica. I made the next logical move and initiated a nationwide search. There were plenty of Greenlaws throughout the United States, three identified specifically as "Jessica."

The first was my match in Plymouth, the second and third showed addresses in Arizona and Indiana. I pulled both entries from the list and requested further information. Moments later, Arizona's version of Jessica Greenlaw showed 1930 as a date of birth. Indiana's was 1983.

I shut off the computer and propped my feet up on the corner of the desk. It was too early for a drink, but I hadn't ruled it out. The worst part of the entire situation was that I suspected nothing nefarious had happened to Jesse. Odds were, she'd played Abdiel for his cash, eventually grown tired of him and decided to scoot.

Of course, most people would make their intentions known and simply move on, but Jesse always had a flair for the dramatic. For her, slipping away without explanation was typical behavior. Since she hadn't touched the bank accounts or run up her credit cards as yet, I figured she must've been squirreling money away prior to her planned departure and was living strictly off cash. But she'd been gone more than a month. Sooner than later, the well would run dry and she'd be forced to tap into other resources, and that's when I'd nail her. Until then I'd do a little legwork and talk to as many people as I could. Experience in missing persons cases had taught me that somebody always knew where the quarry was; it usually boiled down to simply pushing the right buttons.

When I first met her I knew, way back in high school, Jesse was a project. Orphaned at birth, she lived in a series of foster homes—most of them abusive in one way or another—until her eighteenth birthday. Once a legal adult, her flamboyance gave new meaning to the label free spirit. She behaved as if she'd been dealt a lousy hand from the very start, which she had, and planned to spend the rest of her life evening the score. While still in her teens, Jesse realized the power she wielded over men, and had never been afraid to use it. More than a beautiful face and a sinful body, she was driven—focused—and possessed a deviously commanding intelligence. Jesse got what Jesse wanted one way or another, and although for a time I thought she truly loved me, it was years before I understood her love for someone else could never match her uncanny desire for survival and self-gratification.

Now, after meeting Abdiel, I realized I was only one victim on a probable roster of many. In a way, I felt bad for the poor sap. I knew exactly what he was going through and wouldn't wish that sort of agony on my worst enemy.

I glanced back at my notes, focused on the name and address of the film producer I'd been given, and found myself wondering if my car could make it all the way to Hyannis.

Chapter 5

Once the summer dies down, much of Cape Cod becomes little more than a series of ghost towns. Still, the rural setting was a pleasant change from the city, and as I crossed the Sagamore Bridge—an enormous structure of metal and concrete connecting the Cape to the mainland— I found myself a bit more at ease. From New Bedford, Hyannis is about an hour drive. Puttering along in my deathtrap took nearly thirty minutes more, but the time afforded me the chance to prepare for my unscheduled visit with Walter Rizzi.

I found his office just off the highway exit, tucked away behind a strip mall at the farthest end of a spacious parking lot. It was a small, windowless, one-story stucco building with a sign above the double glass front doors which read: LOVESTRUCK PRODUCTIONS. There were only two other cars occupying spaces—a Lexus sedan and a rusty Volkswagen Bug that looked even older than my ride. I grabbed a tie from my glove compartment, quickly wiped it free of crumbs, lint and an assortment of debris and slipped it on. Even dressed in scuffed boots, a pair of faded jeans and a battered leather jacket, there was something about wearing a tie that made me feel smarter, more confident and even a bit righteous. Old Catholic school habits die hard.

I sauntered into the reception area like I owned the place. The red wall-to-wall carpeting was so bright it hurt my eyes, and a bevy of identically framed posters along the outer office advertised a string of adult films with titles and busty actresses straight out of the mind of a hormone-crazed junior high school kid. Just beyond a matching pair of black vinyl couches, a secretary old enough to be my grandmother glanced up from a pile of paperwork on her desk with a questioning stare.

"I'm here to see Walter," I announced with a smile.

The woman reached for a pair of eyeglasses dangling from a chain around her neck and slid them onto the tip of her nose. "And you are?"

"David Drago."

Grandma arched an eyebrow. "Do you have an appointment?"

"No, ma'am," I said with a grin. "I sure don't."

"Then what is this regarding?"

I moved closer to the desk and offered her one of my business cards. She smirked as if it were diseased, so I placed it on the blotter in front of her. Once she'd read it and offered the usual concerned expression the words *Private Investigations* always seem to generate, I said, "Probably be best if I speak with Walter directly."

Her eyes darted about behind the eyeglasses. "I'm afraid Mr. Rizzi is in a very important meeting right now and cannot be disturbed. You'll have to make an appointment."

I started back toward the couches. "I'll wait."

The woman struggled to her feet. "He'll be tied up all afternoon."

"Is that his office?" I asked, pointing to a door marked

"Private" just beyond her desk.

"That's none of your concern." Jowls swayed menacingly as she shook her head. "If you'd like to make an appointment, I'll be happy to—"

Before she'd finished, I was already around the side of her desk. "Why don't I just poke my head in and say hello?"

With the oldest porn queen in history barking out objections and hobbling after me, I opened the office door and stepped inside.

A man with a hideous toupee sat behind an enormous desk, a telephone plastered to his ear. Startled, he reared back as I entered the room. "Can I help you?"

I tried to close the door behind me but the secretary managed to block it with a bony shoulder. "I'm sorry, Walter," she said through labored breath, "he just rushed by me!"

"Lenny," Walter growled into the phone, "lemme call you back." He slammed the receiver onto the cradle and pushed himself into a standing position. He was a few inches over six feet (which made him taller than me), and appeared to be in excellent physical condition for a man in his sixties. "What's this all about? Who are you?"

"Name's Drago." I handed him a business card. "I need to ask you a few questions."

It seemed to take him an inordinate amount of time to read the card. "I don't have to talk to you," he finally said. "Who the hell do you think you are, busting in here? I know you? You think you're somebody? Take off or I'll call the cops."

I smiled at him. "See, now that's just a plain bad idea, Walter."

"It's okay, Ma," he said to the secretary. "I'll take care of this." Once she'd closed the door behind her, he ripped my card in half, tossed it into a wastebasket and glared at me. "You a little soft in the head or something, pal?"

"Don't be silly, Wally. I'm not your pal." I lowered myself into a chair in front of his desk. "Like I said, I just want to ask you a couple questions."

"I'm busy."

"Yeah, I'll bet." I noticed a cigar burning in an ashtray, so I lit a cigarette. "I used to be a cop over in New Bedford."

"Who gives a shit?" Walter put his hands together and cracked his knuckles with a loud pop. "What's wrong with you?"

"I still know quite a few of the guys on the force." I took a lengthy drag and exhaled a cloud of smoke at him. "It'd be a shame if they called their brothers in the Hyannis department and told them they'd heard from a reliable source that you've been using underage models in your little epics."

"That's bullshit." Walter stabbed a finger at the air between us. "Every actress fills out the appropriate forms and shows ID. All my girls are consenting adults and I got the paperwork to prove it. If you think you're gonna come in here and push me around, you're even dumber than you look."

"Okay," I said, making sure to add a dramatic shrug. "But it's amazing how fast you can get a search warrant when minors may be at risk. Wouldn't it suck to spend a whole day watching a bunch of cops dig through your files and trash your place just to make sure?"

He drew a deep breath, nervously adjusted the waistband on his designer sweat suit and drifted back toward his desk chair. "You don't want to threaten me. I got connections."

"I'm sure you do, Wally." I glanced around the office. More posters filled the walls and there were three bookcases lined with hundreds of video cassettes. "You must've pulled a lot of strings to get away with setting up this dump in a town like Hyannis."

He leaned forward, placed his hands on the desk. "You gonna leave or do I have to throw you out?"

"I'm not looking to give you a hard time, Wally. I've got a few questions concerning Jesse Greenlaw I need answers to and I'll be out of your hair...so to speak."

He casually adjusted his toupee, as if to be certain it was still there. "It's Walter."

"Unless, of course, you keep playing the hard-on, in which case I'll be happy to turn into the biggest pain in the ass you've ever seen."

Walter plopped into his chair with a muffled grunt. "You're already in the running for the biggest pain in the ass I've ever seen."

"I do a lot of missing persons stuff. A lot of teens that run away from home and end up in bad situations with bad people. See where I'm going with this? Now I can make a call and report a client with a missing thirteen-year-old daughter has a friend claims she was working for you, or—"

"That's a load of shit!"

"*Or* you can play nice, and we can have a little chat-sky."

"Just ask your fucking questions, all right? I got shit to do."

I took out my pad and pen. "I understand she worked for you a little over a month ago."

"Hey, a lot of people work for me."

"Seems the last time anybody saw her she was wrapping up work on one of your movies. I've been hired to track her down."

"By who?"

"Can't tell you that," I said. "My client wishes to remain anonymous, and I'm obligated to honor that. When's the last time you saw Jesse?"

"I don't remember. She's just another broad with a nice rack and a talent for spit-shining the baloney pony. They're a dime a dozen in my business, know what I mean?"

"You're starting to piss me off." I crushed my cigarette in the ashtray. "You and that dead fucking squirrel you got on your head. Answer the question, Wally. I don't have all day either."

It was obvious from his expression that Walter Rizzi was not accustomed to being spoken to in such a harsh manner. "You really think you got a big set swinging between your legs, don't you? Do you know who I am?"

"Check your license if you're confused. Tell me about the work Jesse did for you."

Walter stuffed his cigar into the corner of his mouth. "Look," he said with a sigh, "I do small, direct-to-video and some internet stuff, all right? I mostly use amateur talent because that's hot at the moment and plus I can't afford the big-name adult stars. Now and then I contract somebody who's done smaller roles for some of the major producers and slap them in a starring part in one of my projects. Jesse Greenlaw—she works as Jesse Hellion—

isn't exactly a name, but she's done a lot of scenes in big-budget films and most hard-core fans know the face, among other things. A while back she worked for a friend of mine in New York and I saw her audition tape. I got her name and number from him."

"She didn't have an agent?"

"Jesse agents herself." The phone rang but Walter ignored it. "She was living over in Plymouth, so I hired her to come in and do some string work."

"What's that?"

"She comes in with the rest of the talent and we shoot a string of scenes, try to get as much footage of her as we can. Later, I can take those hours of film and edit them into dozens of different titles. You know, instead of shooting a single, scripted film."

I couldn't prevent a slight chuckle. "You guys use *scripts*?"

Walter frowned and chomped his cigar. "She worked three days for me about a month and a half ago. I haven't seen or spoken to her since. Didn't have no reason to."

"How was she to work with?"

"She got along with the rest of the cast and crew all right, I guess. See, mostly everybody in the business knows each other—I'm talking the pros here—but a lot of the big-name broads do the strip club circuit. They start getting fan mail and forget they're still just nice pieces of ass that spread their pussies and suck cock and lick pussy for a living. Jesse wasn't like that. She had an ego—everybody in this business does—but she was a pro. Jesse always showed up on time, did her work and went home. She didn't do pain, but that was really her only restriction. She'd do girl-on-girl, take it up the ass, whatever."

I looked up from my pad. "Cool."

"She even did money shots without bitching. The goo shots." Walter smoothed the back of his wig with his free hand. "You know, where the guy blows his load all over some honey's face. We call it the money shot because it's what most fans pay to see, follow?"

"Clever bunch, you porn dudes. Does Jesse have any friends you know of, anyone she associated with on a regular basis?"

"I don't know nothing about her personal life."

"Didn't she make friends with anybody on set?"

"I couldn't say."

"Why not?"

Walter smirked. "Because, ass-wipe, if I went around giving out names and private information on people nobody'd ever work for me. I got privacy rules in my business too, Drago."

"Afraid I'll rat you out?"

"It crossed my mind."

"Don't worry about it. Tell me about her friends."

Walter shifted uncomfortably in his chair. "Look, I've answered everything I'm gonna—"

"I noticed a pay phone over at the convenience store down the street. If I called from there, you'd probably have a room full of curious cops in here before the end of the day. How about it, Wally? You a betting man?"

He smashed his cigar in the ashtray, probably fantasizing it was my face instead, and jerked open a file cabinet alongside his desk. "She was friendly with a chick named Whitney Blue. They'd done films together before and Jesse was comfortable doing girl-girl scenes with her. Whitney's worked for me on and off now for about three years." He recited an address in Boston then slammed the file shut. "You didn't get that information from me."

"You think she might know where I can find Jesse?"

"Ask her."

"You can count on it."

"Like I said, Jesse did a lot of work in New York. She even pulled jobs in Los Angeles and Vegas from time to time. That's probably where she's at." Walter scratched his chin with a gold nugget ring on his pinkie finger. "She's not in trouble, is she?"

I put my pad away and stood up. "I don't know."

"Just make sure you keep me out of it if she is."

"It's my understanding Jesse was planning on leaving the business. Hear anything about that?"

"People come and go in this industry. She never said anything to me about packing it in, but it's possible she'd had enough. Jesse made decent money in the three or four years she worked the biz, and I know she had dreams of being a legit actress. 'Course, that's not unusual."

"Anything else you can tell me about this Whitney Blue?"

A subtle change crept across Walter's face. "I don't know her that well. She works for me sometimes; it's not like we hang out or nothing. Hell, I've never even gotten so much as a blow job off her. She's easy enough to work with, but once the cameras are off she keeps pretty much to herself, which is fine by me. Whitney's a strange kid."

"How so?"

By the time he answered my question, I realized the look of annoyance in his eyes had been replaced with one that more closely resembled fear. "I've never talked to her about it myself, but I've heard the rumors. She's supposedly into some spooky shit."

"Spooky?"

"Some people in the business are into the black arts," he said softly. "Black witchcraft, dark Satanism—that kind of thing."

"Does that include you?"

His eyes found mine. "No, it doesn't. I been a Catholic my whole life. Maybe I don't go to church as much as I—"

"Are you're telling me Whitney Blue's a devil worshipper?"

"I didn't say that." Walter's face contorted into a grimace. "She used to carry tarot cards around with her and give readings to some of the cast and crew while they were on break—harmless shit lots of people do—but I never got involved in any of it. People talk, all right? She claims she's some sort of witch, that it's just a religion like anybody else's and all that, but the rumor going around is that she's a hardcore Satanist." His complexion turned pasty and pale. "If you really want to know the truth, I've heard the same thing about Jesse."

I hoped my surprise wasn't as evident as his apprehension. "That's the first I've heard of that."

"You asked, I told you." He pushed his chair away from the desk and stood up. "Look, I'm a busy man. Are we done here?"

"For now, yeah, we're done."

"Good." Walter strutted across the room like an aging rooster, straightened his wig and opened the door. "Then get the fuck out of here and leave me the hell alone."

Chapter 6

I spent that evening at the office eating Chinese takeout, contemplating my next move and replaying the conversation with Walter Rizzi again and again in my mind. Although I was confident odds were Whitney Blue could tell me where Jesse was hiding, getting her to talk to me if she did know anything was another matter entirely. Threats and strong-arm tactics worked on lowlifes like Rizzi, but likely weren't an option with her.

Thunder rumbled ominously in the distance. The violent showers that had assaulted the area earlier had been replaced by a slow, steady drizzle, and I found myself wondering if it was raining wherever Jesse was.

Don't do it, I scolded myself. *Don't let her back in. Don't let her get a hold on you again.*

I finished my Peking ravioli and chicken fried rice, allowing the rhythm of the rain to distract me. After dark, my building was always as still as a cemetery, but the neighborhood itself seemed unusually quiet. Commercially zoned, the building housed only two other units. A pawnshop that had been there for years occupied the first floor, I was on the second, and the floor above me had been empty since I'd moved in. Across the street was a low-income apartment complex, a gas station and a convenience store. A pizza parlor and an auto parts dealer rounded out the rest of the street's main draws. Most of the remaining real estate consisted of condemned, graffiti-covered structures and vacant, garbage-strewn lots. It was a rough neighborhood, but I'd never had any problems to speak of.

The son of factory workers, I'd grown up less than ten blocks away, and with the exception of my four-year tour in the Army and the ten months I'd spent with Jesse in the nearby town of Dartmouth, I'd lived my entire life in the south end of New Bedford.

Although the city had reached legendary status as the setting of Herman Melville's *Moby Dick*, the modern version retained historical significance but little else. Famous in its heyday for the whaling and textile industries, New Bedford had been reduced in many areas to a rotting shell, a vague memory of what had once been. Littered with enormous, mostly abandoned mills and factories, and growing crime, drug and unemployment problems, the city was compromised of an odd combination of neighborhoods which architecturally blurred the boundaries between its storied past and an attempt at a more contemporary visage. With few exceptions, it was a gray, almost Gothic looking little city, but was primarily populated by a diverse ethnic and economic cross-section of decent, hard-working folk. The city was in the midst of a comeback and major renovations, and the future seemed bright, but either way, I'd been born here, raised in these streets and New Bedford was my home.

My sister had been born and raised here as well, but she'd married and moved to Kansas more than a decade ago, and my parents had long since passed away. I was alone, with no substantive reason to stay. Yet I did. At times my motives—or lack thereof—puzzled even me.

I dug the photograph Abdiel had given me out of my desk drawer and studied it a while. As hedonistic and driven as Jesse was, I couldn't imagine her being involved in anything like hardcore Satanism. She'd never been a particularly religious person, but I could clearly recall conversations we'd had about her personal spiritual beliefs, and while most organized religions would have deemed them self-serving at best, they certainly weren't evil. The concept of her intentionally being involved in something that celebrated evil and darkness was absurd.

My eyes scanned her face, then body. Even now it was the little things I missed most. Her laugh, her scent, the way she'd cling to me in the night, hair fanned out across the pillows and the heat of her breath caressing my bare chest.

"Where are you?" I whispered.

Jesse stared back, frozen in time.

The world turned stark white.

At the farthest reaches of a long and narrow hallway, I saw Jesse standing against the wall in a sheer summer dress, arms folded; her eyes mournful and moist with fear. I started toward her, my slippers scuffing the pristine tile floor, but she didn't seem to notice me.

Before I could reach her, the silence was interrupted by an odd rippling sound, like tattered sails billowing in heavy winds. As the sound grew louder, I hesitated, cinched the belt on my robe and called to her.

Her eyes shifted, became lifeless black pools, empty sockets. "Don't," she gasped. "*Don't!*"

I looked down to see blood—fresh, thick and wet— dripping from my hands.

The sound became deafening, and I suddenly realized what it was.

Wings...

The flapping of enormous, unseen wings...

I awoke to the sound of a telephone ringing. Still slumped over my desk, I pawed at my eyes, fought off a lengthy yawn and checked my watch. It was just after midnight. "Hello?"

"I apologize for calling so late," a whispery female voice said, "but I'm looking for David Drago."

"You got him." I leaned back in my chair, still blinking away sleep and shaking off the effects of the nightmare. "Who's this?"

"Whitney Blue."

Chapter 7

Stunned, I attempted to compose myself and process a sudden maelstrom of disjointed thoughts into some sort of intelligible response.

"Are you there?" she asked.

"Yeah—yes—I'm here."

"I understand you want to talk to me."

"How did you get my number?"

"Shouldn't that be my question?"

"You called me, Ms. Blue."

"According to Walter Rizzi, you forced your way into his office today and were asking questions about Jesse Greenlaw. He said you mentioned me specifically and planned to contact me. I'd like to know how you got my name."

"From my client," I lied.

"Anyone I know?" she asked coolly.

"I'm not at liberty to say." I wanted to see if she'd make the next move. When she didn't, I said, "All I can tell you is that I've been hired to find Jesse."

There was a brief pause before I heard a response. "I didn't realize she was missing."

I could've sworn I felt my pulse quicken. "You know where she is?"

"Well, not exactly, no."

"I thought you were—"

"Look, Mr. Drago, you're not a policeman and I'm under no obligation to answer your questions." She offered a dramatic sigh. "I am, however, willing to talk to you if it's absolutely necessary, but it'll be on my terms or not at all. I won't allow you to harass me the way you did Walter, is that clear?"

"Crystal."

"I don't like to talk on the phone," she said in a more relaxed tone. "I'd rather do this face-to-face and get it over with."

"Just tell me where and when."

"I'll be at *The Deadbolt* tomorrow night. It's a night-club in Boston, ever heard of it?"

"Afraid not."

"It's just off Boylston Street, a few blocks from the Prudential Center. By seven o'clock there'll be a line form-ing on the street, you can't miss it."

I nodded into the phone. "I'll be there."

"Ask for me at the door."

"I appreciate your cooperation," I said. "Let me just ask one more—"

The line clicked.

"Ms. Blue?"

Went dead.

I hung up and rummaged through a nearby file cabi-net until I'd located my vodka stash. I poured myself a double, but it died as quickly as Whitney Blue's phone connection.

Never one to give up without a fight, I defiantly poured another.

Chapter 8

It was mid-afternoon by the time I rolled out of my cot and staggered to the window. The rain had stopped but it was still cloudy and dim.

After a sponge bath, I dressed and went to the pizza joint down the street for lunch, then drove across town to a rental company I often used, and leased a car for the night. I was on the road by six o'clock and arrived in Boston just before seven.

I took the Chinatown exit, passed through the theater district and what was left of the city's infamous Combat Zone—a confederation of adult video stores, peep shows and strip clubs—and eventually turned onto Boylston Street. Even before I'd found a parking space I realized Whitney Blue hadn't been exaggerating.

Starting at the top of an unmarked stairwell which led below street level, located between a convenience store and a used CD shop, a line of more than thirty people had formed. Most were in their early to middle twenties and reminded me of fans I'd once seen at a midnight screening of *The Rocky Horror Picture Show*.

The men were either eel thin or muscle-bound gym rats, both varieties sporting wildly theatrical makeup and dark leather outfits complete with studded collars and boots. The majority of women—pale, with teased hair; eyes, lips and fingernails painted black—followed suit. A multitude of body piercings and an overall vampire-punk-corpse motif seemed to be the current rage.

I approached the crowd from across the street like a mouse whistling his way through a snake's lair, and amidst a volley of objections, cut to the front of the line. An enormous Asian man working the door stepped in front of me. Looking me up and down, he shook his shaved head in apparent disbelief. "Forget it," he said, folding a pair of heavily tattooed arms across his chest. "This ain't your kind of party, my man."

"Yeah, no shit, Schwarzenegger." With the muffled strains of speed metal thudding beneath my feet, I glanced down the staircase. It was dark beyond the first few steps. "Whitney Blue said to ask for her at the door. Tell her David Drago's here to see her."

The man stared at me for several seconds as if weighing the validity of my response, then pulled a flip-phone from his leather chaps and punched in the appropriate numbers. "Ms. Blue? Yeah, it's Sumo. I got a guy out front here who says you're expecting him. Little fella, maybe five-nine, thinning brown hair, goatee…yeah… probably about thirty-two or three, looks like he sleeps in his clothes. Says his name's David Drago, I—yes, ma'am." He snapped the phone shut and jerked a thumb toward the staircase. "Go to the door at the bottom of the stairs. You're gonna see a chain-link fence that runs along the left-hand wall. Follow it to the back until you hit the bar. Somebody will meet you there and take you to Ms. Blue."

"Thanks," I said, moving past him. "And I'm five-ten, you dick."

The music grew louder as I descended the steps, pushed my way through a steel door and stepped directly onto a huge dance floor. Countless people were slam dancing in the relative darkness, the only light provided by pulsing strobes and a series of giant video screens suspended from the ceiling, which showcased a montage of rapid, pornographic images and old black-and-white horror film clips. A pungent cloud of dense smoke thickened the air, and the bare concrete floor was sticky beneath my boots.

The walls were black, making depth and distance difficult to gauge, but I managed to find the fence along the left-hand side of the room and followed it through the mass of jerking bodies. I eventually reached a bar constructed to resemble a gargantuan coffin. A blood-red, five-pointed inverted star was painted directly on the wall above it, and barbed wire had been strung beneath the front counter. A topless male bartender with pierced nipples looked at me, dark eyes shifting through peepholes slashed in his leather hood. He said something, but between the roar of music and a partially closed zipper concealing his mouth, I couldn't hear him. With a shrug, he slid further down the bar to wait on someone else.

I turned, looked back out at the dance floor and watched the sea of ghouls and lost souls jumping about like victims of seizure—Just another Saturday night barn dance in Hell.

A stout man with a blue Mohawk, bad skin and a nose ring connected to a spike through his ear with a silver chain emerged from the crowd. "I need to see some ID!" he screamed, holding his hand out like a bellboy awaiting a tip.

I assumed he wanted to see my investigator's license, but since I hadn't paid the fifteen hundred bucks to renew it in more than a year, I gave him a business card instead. After inspecting it briefly he headed toward the end of the bar and motioned for me to follow.

We slipped through an opening behind the bar and into a narrow hallway, the ceiling arched, round and dimly lit by low-watt bulbs encased in iron bar hoods. The man stopped at the first door we came to. "Go on in," he said with a sneer. "But just so you know, I'll be right outside the whole time."

I faked a shiver, rolled my eyes and entered a small office. Much to my surprise it was modestly decorated. Behind a sprawling desk covered with paperwork sat a woman with long dark hair and a fair complexion. I put her at roughly my age. Dressed in a conservative business suit, Whitney Blue more closely resembled a yuppie accountant than a porn star. Looking up from a calculator tape, she offered a disinterested expression and pointed to one of two chairs positioned in front of her desk. "Have a seat."

I recognized the same hushed voice I'd heard on the telephone. "Ms. Blue?"

"Welcome to *The Deadbolt*, David." She sat back in her leather swivel, crossed her legs and flashed a pearly smile. "You don't mind if I call you *David*, do you?"

"Not at all," I said. "Interesting club you got here."

"It's not for everyone."

"You work here?"

Her dark eyes sparkled with amusement. "I own the place."

"Porno's been berry-berry good to you, huh?"

Unimpressed with my attempt at humor, she retrieved a cigarette from a case on the desk and inserted the filter into an onyx holder. "Quite good, actually."

I noticed a ring on her left hand. Engraved across the flat front surface was an inverted star identical to the giant version I'd seen over the bar.

"I have a silent partner," she added, allowing the words to linger in the air like a curious odor. "But as long as the profits keep rolling in, he generally stays out of the way and I can do what I want."

"Looks like you've got a gold mine going. Why stay in the adult film business?"

"This place takes up most of my time these days. I only work in film occasionally. I went to college, David. I have a business degree. Sorry to shatter your illusions, but we're not all empty-headed bimbos. Unlike a lot of women in the business, I never fucked and sucked for money because I had to, or because I couldn't do anything else."

"You just dig it, huh?"

"I just dig it, David." Whitney slowly traced her upper lip with her tongue, her eyes locked on mine throughout. "But I didn't realize we were here to discuss me."

"So Walter Rizzi warned you that I—"

"Walter's a worm," she said evenly. "He's known me long enough to realize it's never a good idea to be on my bad side. He swears he didn't give you my name but we both know he's lying, don't we, David?"

I ignored her comment. "You said on the phone you didn't realize Jesse was missing."

She took a delicate drag on her cigarette, exhaled through her tiny nose. "I knew she was planning to take off for a while, but as to exactly where she ended up, I haven't a clue."

"I thought you two were close."

She nodded. "We're friends, yes."

"And you expect me to believe she didn't tell you where she was going?"

"What you believe or don't believe makes absolutely no difference to me one way or the other." She flicked a long ash from the tip of her cigarette into an ornate copper ashtray. "Who hired you to find her?"

"I can't tell you that."

A subtle smile crept across her face. "Jesse used to talk about you quite a bit. In a way, I feel as if I already know you. I realize it's probably hard for you to understand, since she left you, but the truth is, she missed you terribly. In the long run, I think she knew she'd made a mistake."

I wasn't about to let her lure me into a conversation about my relationship with Jesse, so I let it go. "You said you knew she was planning to leave. Why?"

"She'd grown tired of the business, among other things, and told me she wanted to go somewhere for a while, get her head together and figure out what to do with her life next."

"And you can't even give me an educated guess as to where she might be?"

Before answering, she studied me with the cold efficiency of a natural predator casually selecting its prey. "Probably somewhere quiet and secluded. The last time we spoke was at the wrap party for Walter's film in Hyannis, and that was more than a month ago. I haven't heard from Jesse since."

"Don't you expect to?"

"I certainly hope I'll see her again, if that's what you're asking." Whitney bent her elbow and held the cigarette up like Bette Davis. "I first met her at a gentlemen's club in Brockton. Jesse was one of the opening acts and I was working the top of the bill as part of a promotional tour for *Bang the Bum Slowly*, a movie I'd recently completed."

"A classic in the annals of film, no doubt. Or should I say *anals*?"

Whitney's attempt at composure was replaced by a dead, vacant stare. "It makes me very angry when people disrespect me, David."

"Just a joke, honey, relax."

"*Honey*? Really?"

"Slipped right out, I'm so embarrassed."

She rolled her eyes.

"Now look what I've done. I've offended the star of *Bang the Bum Slowly*."

"Jesse always said you had a warped sense of humor. More annoying and immature, I'd say."

"And I haven't even gotten to my fart jokes yet."

Her expression softened. "Jesse hadn't been dancing long but she stood out from the other girls. She had definite star quality. We had a few drinks after our sets and became friends. She wanted me to help her break into film."

"You must get requests like that a lot when you work the strip clubs," I said. "What made you want to help Jesse?"

"I felt sorry for her. You'd run off and joined the military, and then the Gulf War broke out. Jesse was terrified you'd be killed and she'd never see you again."

"I didn't realize you'd known her then," I admitted. "We lived together for almost a year after I came home and I don't remember her ever mentioning you."

Whitney scratched the space beneath her nose with a dainty, bird-like finger. "When she heard you were coming back in one piece, she changed her mind about pursuing a film career. She said you were going to have to spend some time in a veterans' hospital but that hopefully your stay there would be a short one."

It felt as if my heart had sunk all the way to my ankles. The few months of transition time I'd spent in the hospital was not something I'd thought Jesse had ever told anyone about.

"Apparently you had some…*psychological* issues you needed to work out," Whitney said with a glint in her eyes. "It must have been awful—terrifying, even—but I take it you're all better now?"

"I had a few adjustment problems," I said through gritted teeth. "Thanks for your concern. You were saying?"

"It was almost a year before I heard from her again. When I did, I took Jesse under my wing. I introduced her to some people, taught her the ropes as best I could and within a few years she was getting almost as much work as I was. Have you seen any of her movies?"

"No."

"Ever seen any of mine?"

"Can't say as I have."

Her eyes searched mine. "I'm not sure I believe you."

"Well, I'm not sure I'm telling the truth." I offered a playful smirk. "So Jesse was doing well in the business, making lots of money, right? What made her suddenly want to walk away from it all?"

"Jesse was driven. She wanted to be a major star—no doubt about it—but in her personal life she was fairly laid back." Whitney paused as if she expected me to ask another question. When I didn't, she said, "A few weeks before she left, she started to act differently."

"How so?"

Whitney looked away. "Something was bothering her. She seemed nervous. I might even go so far as to say frightened."

"Did you ask what was upsetting her?"

"I tried, but she didn't want to talk about it."

"Was she having problems with anyone in the business?"

"Not that I know of."

"Did she have any enemies?"

"Don't we all?"

"Some more than others," I said. "To tell you the truth, I've heard some rumors about your involvement in the black arts. After seeing this place I'm inclined to believe them."

Whitney plucked her cigarette from the holder and butted it in the ashtray. "And your point is?"

"Did you introduce Jesse to those things as well?"

"Look, I don't know what you think I am," she said, "but I'm not some psychotic Satanist if that's where you're going with this."

"Then what's the deal with the ring you're wearing? I don't know much about these things but the last time I checked an inverted five-point star was a satanic—"

"You've seen too many horror movies." Whitney glanced at her ring and laughed lightly. "A pentagram can mean many things, David."

"What's it mean to you?"

"Power." She folded her hands, concealing the ring from view. "I'm a practicing witch and, before you ask, I don't own a pointy black hat, I don't eat babies by moonlight or cast evil spells, and I drive a Volvo, not a broomstick. Witchcraft is a religion like any other. It has nothing to do with Satanism. Get a clue."

"My question was, did you introduce Jesse to these things as well?"

"She had only a passing interest in spirituality." Whitney slid her chair away from the desk and sauntered to a cabinet against the wall. Her figure was slender but dangerously curved in all the right places. I sat silently while she removed a bottle of bourbon from the cabinet shelf. "Like a drink?"

"No thanks."

She poured one for herself, walked around the desk and leaned against the front of it. The closer she got, the more attractive she became. "I don't have to talk to you, David."

"Then why are you?"

Whitney combed a strand of hair behind her ear with a finger. "Regardless of what you may think of me, I do care a great deal for Jesse and, frankly, I'm worried about her. She's on the run from something—what, I don't know—but whatever jam she's gotten herself into surely can't be insurmountable. I don't want you snooping around my business ventures or me but if and when you find her, I'd like to know. I'll help Jesse any way I can."

I sat forward a bit, closing the already small gap between us, and caught a vague trace of her cologne. "How do I know you're not the one she's running from?"

"Don't be ridiculous. What possible reason would Jesse have to run from me? I'm the only friend she's got."

As Whitney sipped her drink, her suit jacket fell open and I glimpsed an inch or two of cleavage above the edge of her blouse. Along the side of one breast was a small tattoo in the shape of a unicorn. When I reestablished eye contact, I realized I'd been caught peeking.

"Dream on," she smirked. "*Honey.*"

"Trust me. They don't make a condom thick enough."

Whitney swirled the amber liquid around in her glass as if trying to determine a suitable punishment for my remark. "None of us are without sin, David. Even you. Some might say, *especially* you."

"They just might."

"I guess we've all got blood on our hands of one kind or another, don't we? But then, I sleep like a baby at night. Do you?"

Instead of answering her question, I asked another of my own. "How was Jesse's relationship with her fiancée?"

Whitney seemed puzzled. "What?"

"Her fiancée," I said again. "How was her relationship with him?"

"I don't—I'm not sure what you mean."

"Isn't it possible she changed her mind, decided she didn't want to get married and just took off on the guy?"

"That doesn't make any sense."

"Why not?"

Whitney frowned. "Because Jesse wasn't engaged."

Chapter 9

The faint squeal of guitars just beyond the confines of Whitney Blue's office momentarily distracted me. The room seemed to darken, and I focused on a small lamp sitting on the corner of her desk. "Maybe you didn't hear," I said. "Jesse had recently gotten engaged to her boyfriend."

Whitney raised an eyebrow. "What boyfriend?"

"The one she was living with in Plymouth."

She stared at me like I'd grown a second head while she wasn't looking. "I don't know where you get your information, but I can tell you that Jesse didn't even have a steady boyfriend, much less a fiancée. I've been to her house in Plymouth dozens of times—it's a nice little rental down on the water—and I know for a fact that Jesse lived alone."

My eyes narrowed as I battled to contain a surge of anger and disbelief. "You're sure of this?"

She put her hands on her hips and shook her head. "Don't you think if Jesse was getting married I'd have known about it? I'm her best friend, for God's sake."

"And you're telling me the house was a rental?"

"You're the detective," she said smugly. "I certainly wouldn't be presumptuous enough to tell you how to do your job, but if you don't believe me simply call the town hall, find out who pays taxes on the property and speak to her landlord directly." Whitney moved behind the desk. "Who told you she was engaged?"

As my mind raced through countless possibilities and scenarios, I tried to downplay my shock. "It was just something I'd heard."

"Someone's deceiving you, David." She dropped into her swivel. "But it isn't me."

If that was true, then my client was a liar. "I appreciate your help," I said, standing. "I won't bother you again."

"You're not so bad," she purred. "After listening to Walter rambling on and on about the hard time you gave him, I was expecting more of a confrontation. You're not what I expected."

Had I been in a better mood I'd have said the same thing about her. "Can I ask you one more thing?"

She folded her hands and placed them on the desk. "Feel free."

"Does the name *Abdiel* mean anything to you?"

Her abrupt change of expression answered the question for me. The blood seemed to drain from her face in a single wave, taking with it the arrogance she had displayed to that point. She swallowed with difficulty, and I noticed her hands had begun to shake. "What name did you say?"

"Abdiel."

"I don't—no, I—it doesn't sound familiar."

"Then why are you rattled?"

"I told you, I—"

"You're lying."

Her eyes bore the look of a caged animal, and somewhere in the back of my mind I thought for the briefest second, I heard her growl like one. "And you're in way over your head if you think you've got what it takes to intimidate me."

"Then what are you afraid of, Whitney?"

The tension in her face gave way to an unsettling stare. "You're the one who should be afraid…so terrified that you can't think, can't move…can't breathe."

I moved closer to the desk. "Luckily for me I don't scare easy, and I don't buy into any of your mumbo-jumbo witchcraft horseshit either, okay? I've been to Hell, lady, and I walked out alive."

An eerie grin pursed her lips. "Maybe you're still there."

"Maybe I don't give a damn."

"I'm very busy. Do let me know if you find Jesse." She reached beneath her desk and I heard a buzzer sound. Before I could say another word the door opened and we were joined by the moron with the blue Mohawk.

He reached for my arm. "C'mon, buddy, meeting's over."

"Keep your fucking hands off me or I'll snap them off at the wrist." When he hesitated I turned back to his boss. "Abdiel. Who is he, Whitney?"

She never gave me an answer, but I knew from the look on her face it wasn't because she didn't have one.

Chapter 10

I headed back to New Bedford angry and confused. I'd allowed the money Abdiel was paying to cloud my judgment and common sense, and was tempted more than once to pull over and kick myself in the ass. Both Walter Rizzi and Whitney Blue had asked who my client was. That in itself should've registered as a red flag. If Jesse had truly been engaged and living with a man for the two years prior to her sudden disappearance, wouldn't it stand to reason that her fiancée was the one who had employed me?

Although my client had lied regarding his specific role in Jesse's life, Whitney definitely knew who he was, and the fact that she'd been frightened at the mere mention of his name was significant. Those things that Whitney Blue genuinely feared more than likely constituted a short list, yet Abdiel obviously made the cut.

The rain was back, accompanied by a stiff, icy wind and intermittent flashes of lightning. I parked the car, scurried across the street to the front steps of my office and fumbled for the appropriate key. Once inside the foyer, I was confronted by an intrusive feeling that I was no longer alone. I switched on the hallway light to better see the staircase leading to the second floor, then turned and looked back out at the street from which I'd come.

Nothing…

My eyes scanned the cars along both curbs, parked into uniform rows like vast metallic headstones, then shifted to the apartment building across the street. A vague silhouette huddled beneath an overhang in the architecture made a subtle but unmistakable move, and a chill lapped the nape of my neck.

Through a haze of darkness and rain, the figure slowly approached me. Stepping onto slick pavement, it paused and I was able to discern a man in a black fedora and matching trench coat, his face concealed in shadow.

I slid my hand into my coat pocket and lied. "I've got a gun."

"So do I," the man answered. "Hopefully neither one of us will have to use them…at least not on each other."

The anxious cadence of his voice was familiar, but I couldn't quite place it. "What do you want?"

"We need to talk, Drago. There isn't a whole lot of time."

And then it clicked. I moved down a step, squinting at the night. "*Walter?*"

He crossed the street, stopped at the base of my steps and allowed the light from the hallway behind me to partially illuminate his face. Weary, bloodshot eyes peered up at me from beneath the brim of his hat. "Can I trust you?"

"Probably not."

"I'm serious."

"So am I."

"I'm not playing games, asshole." He looked up and down the street then turned back to me. "You've got no idea what you're mixed up in here."

"Then explain it to me."

"Not here." He motioned to the staircase. "We need to get off the street."

I kept him in front of me as we climbed the stairs, my heart racing with anticipation, then unlocked the door to my office and escorted him in.

Walter glanced around at the mess. "Jesus, you *live* in here, or what?"

"Yeah, I sort of do." I went directly to my file cabinet and grabbed a bottle of vodka. "Let's have a drink."

He nodded and removed his fedora, careful not to wrest his wig free along with it, and stood quietly near my desk. When I handed him the drink, he cupped the glass with both hands and finished it in a single gulp.

"What's this all about?" I asked.

Although the vodka was gone, he continued to clutch the glass with both hands. "You went to see that bitch tonight, didn't you?"

"Whitney?"

He glared at me. "She thinks I gave you her name."

"You did."

"But you swore you wouldn't—"

"Take a pill. Far as she knows, my client turned me on to her. She's the one who brought your name up, not me." I was already bored with the direction our conversation had taken. "It's the middle of the night, man, what are you doing here?"

"I'm trying to help, you stupid bastard."

"Why would you want to help me all of a sudden?"

He bowed his head. "I've spent my whole life doing things I should've stayed clear of. This time I want to do what's right. It's probably my only chance."

"For what?"

"Salvation."

I leaned against the desk, arms folded. "You need to start making sense or I'm going to bed."

Walter gave a defeated nod and began to pace near the window. "Jesse took off on purpose."

"Want to hold my attention? Tell me something I don't know. Whitney already admitted Jesse was on the run from something, but she didn't know what."

"She told you that?" He seemed to think about his response before continuing with it. "Unbelievable. They must not be able to find her. That means they're hoping you will."

"*They?*"

Walter held his glass out. "Can I get another one?"

I grabbed the bottle from my desk and tossed it to him. "Help yourself."

He poured with trembling hands. "The last day Jesse worked for me she showed up late, looked like death warmed over and was scared out of her mind. We were waiting for her on the set when the makeup girl came out and told me Jesse didn't want to work. Hell, it was the last day of shooting but we still had two scenes to do and Jesse was in both of them. It would've meant shutting down production for an entire day and I couldn't afford to do that.

"I went into her dressing room," he continued, "figuring I'd be able to talk her into working. I wasn't that close to Jesse personally, but she was a pro and knew how to play the game. She had a reputation for taking care of producers, directors, investors—whatever—didn't mind if you wanted some head now and then or wanted to test the merchandise, you see what I'm saying?"

He was making me nauseous. "If there's a point to this feel free to get to it."

"At first, she wouldn't tell me what the problem was," he said. "I kept working on her, telling her whatever it was maybe I could help, you know? But she started crying and said there wasn't nothing anybody could do to help her. I was about to give up when she finally broke. The words came gushing out so fast I could barely understand her. It was like she'd been holding them in for so long once she started talking about it, she couldn't stop.

"She told me she'd gotten into trouble," Walter said. "There was some guy she'd met through Whitney Blue a few years before. I can't remember the guy's name, but it was weird."

"Abdiel?" I asked.

"No, I think it started with a B."

"Do you know anyone by the name Abdiel?"

"It don't ring no bells."

I believed him. "Go on."

"Jesse told me she'd made some sort of business deal with this guy back when she'd first met him, and now it was time for her to pay up." He sipped his drink. "A lot of people hang around the biz and try to get the talent to invest their money in this or that, you know, so it didn't sound that unusual. Only, Jesse was terrified of this guy. She said she couldn't pay him off and didn't have no choice but to run. I offered to hook her up with my lawyer but she looked at me like I was nuts. Since she'd told me this guy was a friend of Whitney's, I asked her how come Whitney couldn't help her out—them being so close and all—but Jesse just kept crying and saying I didn't understand. At that point, I figured there was no way she'd be able to work. I was all set to shut down when Whitney walked in to see what the problem was.

"Just like that," Walter said with a snap of his fingers, "Jesse started acting like it was no big deal. All of a sudden, she just had a little headache and needed a few minutes to pull herself together." Walter looked at me. "The second Whitney left the room Jesse made me swear I'd keep my mouth shut about what she'd told me. That's when I knew this guy wasn't the only one she was afraid of."

"Did you ever question Whitney about this?" I asked.

A humorless laugh escaped him. "I stay clear of the slut. She's got a following—a fan base that helps sales—but unless we're talking business, I don't have nothing to do with her."

"Are you afraid of her?"

"Aren't you?"

"Not particularly, no."

"You ought to be." He took a deep breath, exhaled gradually. "I'm trying to tell you Whitney Blue is more than just some oddball slut. I always knew there were bad people in this world, Drago, but I never really believed in evil until I met her."

Normally I would have dismissed such histrionics, but Walter didn't strike me as the melodramatic type. "She told me she's a witch," I said. "It's a religion, like any other, totally misunderstood, she said."

"She's a whole lot more than that. She ain't no Wiccan, Drago. There's plenty of people into witchcraft who are misunderstood, but this is different." Walter finished his drink, reached for the bottle then changed his mind.

"People like you and me have our differences, but we pray to God. Whitney prays to the other guy."

"You got proof of that?"

"It's common knowledge in the business. She's a high priestess—or some shit like that—in a big satanic church up in Boston. Supposedly all kinds of people are involved in it, from powerful and famous to regular working stiffs. Fucking freaks are everywhere. I heard the rumors about Whitney for years but I never really believed it until Jesse blurted it out herself. This guy she owed was into it too."

"So they dress up in capes and hoods—chant, have orgies, drink piss, fuck chickens, listen to bad music—whatever," I said. "What's any of that got to do with Jesse owing this clown some money?"

Walter rubbed his eyes. "Let me explain something to you, Drago. Because of the work I do, I got to rub elbows with some pretty serious people from time to time. I'm talking about guys that'll put a bullet in your brain and toss you in a trunk just for looking at them a certain way. Sometimes I got no choice but to do business with these people and, like anything else, you get used to it. But Whitney Blue, this other asshole and the people they run with are different, you hear me? They're not just dangerous, they're *damned*."

"Oh, for Christ's sake, Walter. You don't really believe that, do you?"

"I admit I'm not the most religious guy in the world," he said softly. "But I do believe in God. And if there's a God…then there's got to be a Devil."

"Who says?" I lit a cigarette, grabbed the bottle and poured myself another drink. Rain pounded the windows as the building creaked against a mounting wind. "Do you think Jesse was one of them?"

"She might've dabbled in it," he said, "but she was too scared to be a heavy hitter like Whitney. I've never seen nobody so scared."

"Why the hell didn't you tell me all this the other day?"

He stared into his empty glass as if hoping to find the answer there. "I didn't want to get involved in this—I still don't—but Jesse's a good kid, and I've never been able to get the look on her face that day out of my mind. I had to do something."

"If she's really on the run from these people, I'll never find her. Christ, she could be anywhere."

"There might be—" Lightning blinked, startling Walter from the window to the center of the room. He blushed and tendered a spasm-like smile. "I, ah…I'm a little jumpy over here," he said. "Look, there might be somebody else who knows something, but I can't tell you until I know for sure who you're working for."

"I can't—"

"Then how do I know you're not working for one of them?" he snapped. "And how do you know you're not leading them right to her without even realizing it?"

It was a good point, and my loyalty to Abdiel no longer seemed a valid issue. "Do you know if Jesse was engaged?"

Walter laughed dismissively. "She wasn't even seeing anybody that I know of. Jesse never let people get too close, you know? It was like she considered herself bad luck or something."

"I already asked you if you know anyone named Abdiel," I said. "You told me you don't."

"That's right."

"He's my client."

"Who is he?"

"Claims to be Jesse's boyfriend, says they're engaged."

"He's lying."

"I know he is."

"Then he's probably in with them."

"I don't think so. When I mentioned his name to Whitney, she damn near pooped her pants. Whoever he is, she doesn't want anything to do with him." I went to the window where Walter had been standing, gazed out at the night and wondered if it were gazing back. "You let me worry about him. Who is this other person that might know something?"

After what seemed an eternity, Walter said, "His name's Randy Wallace. He used to work for me before he hit it big in fag flicks. Freaking trouser snake on this kid the size of my arm, no lie. Anyway, Randy did a couple of movies with Jesse when she was first starting out, and I know they were friends. If there's anybody else she'd turn to, anybody else she could trust, it's him."

I killed my drink. "Where do I find him?"

He handed me a slip of paper. "Randy made a lot of money, and his boyfriend or whatever he is had big bucks, owns real estate all over New England. He'd be able to offer her plenty of places to hide."

I read the name and an address in Providence, Rhode Island scribbled across the paper. "I'll check it out."

"You do that," Walter said, pulling the fedora back down over his wig. "I don't have anything going on for a while so I'm getting the hell out of here. Gonna take a vacation and lay low. Maybe when I get back this'll all be over."

I watched him remove a small caliber revolver from his coat pocket, quickly check the cylinder then snap it back into position with a flick of his wrist. "Any of them bastards come looking for me they're gonna get some of this," he said, waving the gun at me.

The night had taken on a surreal edge, but the emergence of the weapon brought everything crashing back to stone-cold reality. "Put that thing away before you hurt yourself."

"If they find out I was here tonight," he said, "Jesse's not gonna be the only one they're after."

"Walter, listen to yourself. Just because these people are into some crazy shit doesn't mean they're murderers."

He returned the gun to his pocket. "You got balls, Drago, and I respect that. But you better get your head out of your ass and start taking what I'm telling you seriously. If they find Jesse before you do, they'll kill her. If they find out I helped you, they'll try to kill me. Either way, you're as far from being safe as you can get. I can't make it no plainer than that."

"You can't tell me anything more about this business deal she was involved in?" I asked.

"Jesse never told me no specifics," he said. "All I know is that it was an investment deal that went bad."

"But Jesse made good money," I reminded him. "Paying off a business investment gone sour shouldn't have been that big of a crisis. She must be into this guy for an awful lot of cash. Enough to make her feel she had no choice but to run."

Walter gave a sullen nod. "And enough for this guy to want to kill her once she did."

I waited until he crossed the room and opened the office door before stopping him. Whether it was true or not, there was no question he believed he'd put his life in danger by coming to see me. "Hey, Walter?" He looked back over his shoulder at me. "Thank you."

"I'll see you around, Drago." He buttoned his coat and stuffed his hands deep into the pockets of his trench coat. "Don't forget to say your prayers tonight, you hear?"

Chapter 11

I spent the remainder of Saturday night and the early morning hours of Sunday searching various internet services and every program I owned that specialized in locating people, but failed to come up with any information on Abdiel. When those avenues came up empty, I rifled through several telephone books covering the entire state of Massachusetts and even consulted my reverse phone log—a book used primarily by police departments, collection agencies and private detectives. It lists addresses and phone numbers first, and the names they're registered to second.

Using Jesse's last known address I managed to find the corresponding phone number, but her name was the only one on the account. When I tried calling it, a recorded voice informed me that the number had been disconnected and no further information was available. Just like everywhere else I turned, there was no mention of Abdiel. It was as if the sonofabitch didn't exist or, perhaps, never had. Yet I knew he was planning to contact me first thing Monday morning, and I wanted to be prepared for what was sure to be a confrontational meeting.

I decided against sleep and left for Providence, hopeful that Randy Wallace was the solid lead I'd been waiting for.

* * *

Thunder growled from heavens endless and black.

A forked spear of lightning stabbed the horizon, vanished into curtains of night as torrents of freezing rain bled from a wounded sky.

I was absorbed into darkness; my screams muffled by the din of the storm, and I found myself standing at the rear of a church. I listened to the beat of my heart as it thumped in my chest, felt the blood pulsing through my veins, and inhaled the aroma of scented wax. Soothing, familiar faces of stained glass watched over me, and the fear subsided.

Abdiel stood at the altar, the flickering flames of Pentecostal candles on either side of him providing the only light. He raised his hands, revealed open palms and slowly nodded to me.

"Do you love her?" he whispered.

The steady toll of a distant bell slowly became laughter echoing along the cathedral ceiling, and I noticed another man sitting in a nearby pew. He was old, with a sagging nose, pockmarked skin and black eyes. Lifeless...inhuman...bottomless eyes...His gray hair had receded to the extent that his face consisted almost entirely of forehead, the few remaining strands in front pushed straight back into place and still damp from the strokes of a wet comb. His opaque eyes offered an eerie reflection.

Drawn closer, I allowed the darkness to swallow me.

Staggering along a narrow hallway, I was short of breath and nauseous, knife-like pains firing from my groin across my abdomen. At the far end was an open door, something dangling precariously from the top of the door frame, glinting now and then as it turned and swayed with each step I took.

A cross—a hanging cross—upside down and swaying from a silver chain smeared with blood. I came to an abrupt stop and fell against the wall, watching it swing back and forth like a pendulum. A rancid smell drifted from beyond the small cross, from somewhere beyond the doorway.

I pushed off from the wall, knocked the cross away with a backhand and lurched through to a room bathed in white. The floors, walls, ceiling—all white—seemed to close in around me as my feet slipped and I nearly fell. I looked down and saw a smear of blood next to my foot, so strange there against the pure white. Crouching, I followed the smear across the floor to another door at the far end of the room. The hideous smell grew worse.

The room beyond was a small, cramped bathroom—old, neglected, forgotten. Filthy cracked tiles—some missing entirely—covered the blood-stained floor, the gray walls were spattered with excrement and other foul matter, the wallpaper was peeling or torn free in most places, and the ceiling was low, dingy, and sported numerous cracks and water stains.

A swarm of large flies buzzed about noisily. A small sink and ancient toilet slowly overflowed with gurgling brown water so thick it was nearly gelatinous, the fluid slapping tile with a sickening sound as my eyes followed it to the bathtub against the far wall. A freestanding model, it too was laden with grime along its outer walls. But as I moved closer, my feet sliding along tile, I realized it was filled with an ocean of dark crimson.

"Christ." I gagged, covering my mouth with both

hands as my eyes watered.

A body—small, childlike—floated and bobbed near the surface, its chest an open cavity, its limbs twisted and turned at impossible angles.

As if falling from the edge of a cliff and looking upward while plummeting, I was suddenly hurtling backwards, away from the room, away from the blood and filth and madness.

I blinked, and then again. I'd been staring into the old man's eyes all along.

He retracted pallid lips to expose rotting gums and teeth filed to knifelike points.

"Will you die for her?" he asked in a gurgling voice. "Will you *burn* for her?"

Wiper blades squeaked across the windshield, rain drummed the steel roof and water sluicing off the window to my left dulled the approaching city skyline. I gripped the wheel and shook my head in an attempt to dislodge the cobwebs, still uncertain if I'd been daydreaming or if I'd actually fallen asleep while driving. Shaken, disoriented and increasingly paranoid, I blinked away a bead of sweat and assured myself I hadn't gone crazy. Again.

As I crossed into Providence, disjointed memories of the time I'd spent in the VA hospital seeped to the forefront of my mind. It had only been five years, yet my recollections of that period were ambiguous at best. Much like the combat experiences that led to my hospitalization, I buried the memories of recovery so deeply that even on those rare occasions when I felt inclined to analyze them, they often remained infuriatingly aloof.

I found Randy Wallace's building a few blocks from the civic center. It was an exclusive high-rise with a spacious parking lot full of expensive, mostly foreign cars and a doorman in full regalia standing guard beneath an awning over the entrance. I sat in my shit-box feeling inferior, jealous or just plain indignant—not sure which—and decided to get my head together before venturing inside.

Two cigarettes later I dashed through the rain and took refuge under the awning. The doorman raised a pair of white bushy eyebrows and summoned an enthusiastic smile. "Good afternoon, sir. May I help you?"

"Can you call up to Randy Wallace's place and let him know David Drago is here to see him, please?"

He frowned and scratched his cheek with a gloved hand. "You're looking for Mr. Wallace?"

"Yeah, Randy Wallace lives here, doesn't he?" While the man stared at me like I was speaking in tongues, my patience decided to wait in the car. "Think we can do this today, chief? I'm freezing my balls off out here."

"I'm sorry, sir, but I'm afraid I can't do that."

"What's the problem?"

"It isn't possible. There's been a terrible accident."

I stared at him, waiting.

"Mr. Wallace is no longer with us," he said softly. "He was killed the night before last."

Chapter 12

I stood gawking at him, the breath from my open mouth cloaking the doorman's face in thick clouds of mist as it hit the frigid air.

"Are you all right, sir?" He reached out and gently grasped my arm. "I take it you were a friend of Mr. Wallace's?"

"Yes," I said without thinking. "What happened?"

The doorman released me. "Mr. Wallace was taking his evening walk—he often went for a stroll after dinner—and as he stepped from the curb he was struck by a hit-and-run driver not two blocks from here. Witnesses said the car came out of nowhere and never even slowed down, left Mr. Wallace collapsed in the street like a... well, sir, like I don't know what. Imagine. Makes you wonder just what kind of a world we're living in, doesn't it? Probably some punk hopped up on the crack or something."

"Jesus." I shook my head, not as an intended response but more as a means of clearing it. I'd always been far too cynical to trust coincidence. "When did you say this happened?"

"Night before last, sir." The doorman shuffled his feet against the cold. "It was quite a shock to us all."

I looked back at the parking lot and surrounding

streets, unable to shirk the sudden feeling that we were being watched. As I scanned the area each person hurrying by became suspect, every passing or parked car a potential threat.

The doorman's dour voice distracted me. "A dog doesn't deserve to die like that, much less a kind and decent man like Mr. Wallace."

"Do the police have any leads?" I asked.

"Nothing yet, but I hope they nail the bastard. Pardon me, sir, it's just that Mr. Wallace was always very good to me." He folded his hands and placed them against the front of his thighs. "He and Mr. Niedermeyer both."

"Mr. Niedermeyer?"

"Yes, Kevin Niedermeyer," he replied, and then gauging my expression explained, "Mr. Wallace's roommate."

"Is he at home?"

"Yes he is, but he asked not to be disturbed. I'm sure you understand."

Odds were, Niedermeyer couldn't tell me anything I didn't already know, but I figured it was worth a shot. "You better tell him I'm here anyway."

"As I said, Mr. Niedermeyer cannot be disturbed."

"I'm a private detective," I told him. "It's important."

"Do you work for Mr. Niedermeyer's law firm?"

"Yes, I do."

He smiled patiently. "Are you working in conjunction with the police?"

"No, look—"

His mouth curled into a deprecating frown. "Leave your business card," he said in a tone no longer accommodating. "I'll see that Mr. Niedermeyer gets it."

I reached for my wallet, removed a card and purposely

dropped a twenty-dollar bill in the process. We both saw it spiral to a dry section of pavement shielded from the rain by the awning, but neither of us broke eye contact.

The doorman held out his hand. As I placed my business card in his palm I nonchalantly glanced at his feet and smiled. "Hey, twenty bucks. You must've dropped it."

"Can't be mine," he said smoothly. "I only carry fifties."

I bent down, picked up the bill and stuffed it into his coat pocket. "That's just for getting him on the phone. Tell him an old friend of Randy's is here to pay his respects. Make it out like you can't get rid of me. If he agrees to see me, I'll come across with the rest."

He headed toward the front entrance, hesitated at double doors of tinted glass and looked back at me. "Come wait in the lobby," he said, raising caterpillar-like eyebrows. "We wouldn't want you to freeze your balls off, *chief*."

At the front desk, the doorman had a brief and muffled conversation on the telephone before relieving me of another thirty dollars and escorting me to the elevator. Twelve floors later I found myself standing outside Kevin Niedermeyer's apartment.

A young Hispanic maid answered the door and, with the skill of a seasoned funeral director, gestured for me to enter. "Please," she whispered, "come in."

I stepped onto a high-gloss floor in the entryway and noticed a fresh, fragrant aroma. Stone sculptures sat atop pedestals on either side of the entrance, and a low marble table just beyond was covered with a bevy of lavish floral arrangements.

"May I take your coat?" the maid asked.

"That's all right," I said, duplicating her hushed tone, "I'd rather hang on to it if you don't mind."

She seemed puzzled by my response but gave a morose nod and motioned toward the end of the foyer. "Mr. Niedermeyer is waiting for you."

I thanked her and walked through an arched doorway into a living room larger than any apartment I'd ever rented. The entire rear wall was made of glass and offered a spectacular view of the city, despite the foul weather. Logs burned in an ornate fireplace to my right, and the third wall housed a built-in stereo system worth thousands. Track lights strategically installed along the high ceiling illuminated a plush off-white carpet, various pieces of designer furniture and a handful of modern paintings interspersed with a few originals. The room was breathtaking, yet so pristine that it more closely resembled a museum than an actual living space.

A man sitting on a leather sofa with a drink in his hand looked over at me. His hair was blond and wispy, and a pair of glazed eyes encircled with dark rings ruined an otherwise handsome face. Like the proverbial bull in a china shop, I cautiously moved deeper into the room. "Mr. Niedermeyer?"

He stood up and approached me, his gait fluid, elegant. A double-breasted, charcoal-gray Armani pinstripe enhanced the lines of his lean build, and I suspected that under more normal circumstances Kevin Niedermeyer was a man who possessed tremendous self-confidence and charm. Even in his present condition, he carried himself with the flair of a politician, perhaps a movie star.

"I'm very sorry for your loss," I said quietly.

"Thank you." He gave a joyless smile and shook my

hand.

"Do the police have anything to go on at all?"

"Just that the car was a blue BMW two-door with tinted windows, probably stolen."

"Let's hope that's enough."

"Forgive me, Mr. Drago," he said. "Your name is familiar but I can't seem to place it. The doorman said you knew Randy."

The pain in his eyes prevented me from lying. "Well... no."

Kevin exhaled with a sigh. "I don't understand."

"I'm a private investigator." He stared at me without comment. "I'm trying to locate Jesse Greenlaw."

The muscles in his face slackened. "That's where I've heard the name. You were Jesse's boyfriend at one time."

"Yes."

"She mentioned you in conversation quite frequently."

"I know this is a difficult time, Mr. Niedermeyer, and I'd never intrude if it wasn't absolutely necessary, but Jesse's disappeared. I believe she may be in a great deal of danger, and obviously I can't help her if I don't know where she is. I'm hoping you do."

He nodded. "I'd like to see some identification if you don't mind."

I handed him a business card along with my driver's license, both of which he inspected then returned to me. "Since Randy was one of Jesse's few friends, I figured she might have come to him for help. If there's anything you can tell me, anything at all, Mr. Niedermeyer—"

"Call me Kevin." He pointed to a chair across from the couch he'd been sitting on when I'd first seen him. "Please, sit down. Would you like a drink?"

"It's a bit early for me."

Kevin glanced at his watch. "Yes. Maybe some coffee then?"

"I'm fine. Really." He sank onto the edge of the sofa like a slowly deflating balloon. "I'm sorry we had to meet under such unpleasant circumstances," I said, "but I don't have anywhere else to turn."

He made a steeple with his hands and rested his chin on the tips of his fingers. "Tell me what you know."

"Only that Jesse had some business dealings with a man she met through a friend. Apparently, it had to do with an investment that went bad. Since Jesse made good money and obviously felt she had no choice but to run, she must owe this guy a serious chunk of change. Beyond that, I'm totally in the dark on this."

Kevin listened intently to what I'd said, his bloodshot eyes never leaving me. "And has someone hired you to conduct this investigation, or is it something you're doing on your own?"

"The latter," I said, hopeful he'd bought it.

"Originally Jesse was more Randy's friend than mine. They met while making a…film…for lack of a better word. In time I met her and she began socializing with us as a couple, but by that point she and Randy had known each other for quite a while. Jesse was the only person I ever met from Randy's past I genuinely liked. Still, I could never understand how two people with their brains continued to allow themselves to be degraded and exploited like that. God knows neither of them needed the money."

He waved his hand as if swatting the words from the air. "Randy finally left the business about two years ago.

That was the happiest day of my life." He paused long enough to sip his drink. "We didn't see as much of Jesse after that. Randy and I began to invest heavily in real estate and he assumed the day-to-day management of our properties. I'm an attorney, so I wasn't able to dedicate as much time to those projects as I would have liked, but Randy had an amazing business sense, an uncanny ability to evaluate the market and find the right properties at the right price. What's more, he always knew when to buy and when to sell."

"How long were you two together?" I asked.

"Twelve years." For the first time, he displayed defensive annoyance instead of sorrow. "Does that surprise you?"

"Should it?"

"I'm sorry." He blushed and turned away. "That was uncalled for."

An awkward silence followed before he spoke again. "You work and sweat and sacrifice to make a good life… and then someone comes along and senselessly destroys everything in the time it takes to draw a breath." His eyes filled with tears. "And do you know what the worst part is? The sort of person who could run down another human being with their car and keep right on going like they'd done little more than hit a bump in the road is exactly the sort of person I defend in court on a regular basis. If they have top dollar, of course, no charity counselor, me. Some people would call that final justice for someone who's conducted his life as I have."

"They'd be wrong."

He continued as if he hadn't heard me. "I'm forty-three years old. I made full partner at my firm while still in my thirties, and had found a man with whom I fully intended to spend the rest of my life. I should have realized things were too good to be true."

Surprised that he'd opened up to me so quickly regarding such personal matters, I struggled to find an appropriate response. I came up empty. Despite the state Kevin was in, he was a seasoned, highly successful defense attorney who would not be easily maneuvered. My approach would not only have to be delicate, but cautious, as I didn't want to provide him with even the slightest inkling that I suspected Randy's death might not have been an accident.

"What will you do now?" I asked.

"Get gloriously drunk, for starters." He finished his drink and gazed at the crackling fire, the flames reflected in his glassy eyes. "We hadn't heard from Jesse in a couple of months. I came home one evening and Randy said she'd called and was planning to drop by. He was very concerned because she said she was in trouble but couldn't discuss particulars over the telephone.

"When she got here, I was stunned. Jesse looked terrible, like she hadn't slept in days. She sat right there," he said, pointing to my chair, "and told us she was afraid for her life and needed a place to stay for a while. It all seemed so bizarre I thought at first that she might have had some sort of emotional breakdown. We tried to comfort her, to assure her that whatever the problem was we could help, but she insisted there was nothing anyone could do for her."

I sat forward. "Do you remember exactly what she said?"

He nodded. "She mentioned the business deal you

spoke of earlier. Apparently she'd met this man through a friend several years before and invested with him. Jesse said he'd deceived her. I suggested the best bet was to let me represent her, drag this guy into court and handle things legally. I asked to see whatever paperwork she had regarding the deal, but she kept saying I didn't understand. She explained this man wasn't one who moved in legal circles and that involving a lawyer or the police, was far too dangerous.

"Randy never met you, but from past conversations we'd had with Jesse we knew you were someone very special to her. He suggested she get in touch with you, thinking maybe you could help, but Jesse was reluctant to involve anyone else, especially someone she cared for, and told us the less we knew about all this the better. All she wanted was a place to hide for a while, and since we own several properties across New England, coming to us made perfect sense.

"We let her use our cabin in New Hampshire. It's not far over the Massachusetts border in a secluded, peaceful little town called Bolton. It was exactly what she was looking for. Randy and I spend a...." his voice trailed off into silence. "...We *used* to spend a few weekends a year there. Bolton is the kind of place where people keep to themselves and mind their own business. We were confident Jesse could stay at the cabin without anyone knowing she was there."

"When was this?"

"Four weeks ago," Kevin said. "A few days before Randy's death, Jesse phoned, thanked us and said she was moving on."

"Did she give you any indication of where she might

be headed next?"

"I'm afraid not, no."

I clenched shut my eyes as hope gave way to frustration. "Is there anyone else she might turn to for help?"

"Not really, no. As you said, Jesse had few friends."

"Has anyone else contacted you regarding her whereabouts?"

"Just you."

"What about Randy?"

"If anyone approached him, he would've told me." Kevin stared at me as a dark thought dawned across his face. "Do you think what happened to Randy had anything to do with the people Jesse was running from?"

"No, of course not," I insisted. "How could they have known Jesse had even been here?"

"How did you?"

"Kevin, even if these people are capable of murder, what reason would they have to harm Randy?"

He looked away but I could tell he hadn't yet dismissed the idea. "The police told me the witnesses didn't seem to think the driver hit him purposely," he said, more to himself than me. "But…"

"Do you honestly believe Jesse's life is in danger?" I asked.

Like the good lawyer he was, Kevin paused to consider his answer, as if preparing to disclose a crucial piece of evidence to an unsuspecting jury. "Let me put it this way: People love to slam lawyers, but when they're in trouble the first thing they do is secure the best defense attorney they can afford. I deal with people under tremendous stress every day," he said. "Some wrongly accused, some not. In my line of work guilt or innocence is fundamentally irrelevant, but I've been around long enough to recognize when someone is telling the truth. Jesse was backed into a corner, about as deep into a corner as one can get. To say she was terrified of this man would not be an understatement. I only wish she would've let us do more than provide a temporary hideaway."

I was dying for a cigarette but didn't see any ashtrays. "Did Jesse mention any specific names?"

"I remember Randy asked if he knew this friend who had first introduced her to the man she made the investment with," he said. "I recall the name because it struck me funny at the time. Whitney Blue."

"Did Randy know her?"

"He did, though I'd never met her myself. Later, when he explained she was someone they had both worked with in the past, it was obvious he didn't think too highly of her." He squinted, focusing on memories. "Randy wasn't surprised in the least that Whitney would know someone like this man Jesse was so afraid of. Apparently she was a practicing hardcore Satanist, and he could never understand why Jesse maintained a friendship with her in the first place."

"I never knew Jesse to be involved in that sort of thing," I said, testing the waters.

"According to Randy, Jesse's relationship with Whitney was based more on loyalty than anything else. It was my understanding since Whitney had helped her break into the business Jesse felt indebted to her and often overlooked her rather unsavory religious interests."

"What about the man who was after her?" I pressed. "Was he into this stuff as well?"

"Oh, I couldn't say. The only reason I know Whitney

Blue was caught up in that nonsense was because Randy told me."

"Did she ever give you his name?"

"At one point, yes." He brought a hand to his head and massaged his temples. "It was peculiar, I remember that much. An Arabic name, I believe."

"Abdiel?" I asked through a hard swallow.

"No," he replied quickly. "It began with a B."

Walter Rizzi had said the same thing. I wet my lips, took several deep breaths and feigned patience while he searched his mind.

"Bareth…Babeth…Bal…Balbeth." Kevin rose to his feet and wandered over to the back wall, gazing out at the skyline as he continued to work various combinations aloud. "Balberith," he said finally, facing me. *Balberith.*"

I removed my pad and jotted down the name, spelling it the way it sounded. "Is that a first or last name?"

"I assumed it was his last but I'm not sure."

"And this name meant nothing to either of you?"

"No."

"Do you think Jesse might try to contact you again?"

"Probably at some point," he said, and then, as if the thought had just occurred to him, added, "My God, she'll be devastated when she hears what's happened."

I joined him at the window. "Again, I'm sorry to have bothered you at a time like this."

He managed a thin smile. "I hope I've been some help."

"Absolutely, and if there's anything I can do, you have my card. Don't hesitate to give me a call. If you think of anything else that might be of value, please let me know."

"Jesse made Randy and me promise we wouldn't tell anyone she'd come to us for help," he said, looking directly into my eyes. "But there's been enough pain and suffering. Should I hear from her again I'll contact you immediately. Whatever Jesse's facing, she shouldn't be going it alone." We shook hands. "It's a terrible thing... being alone."

I replied with a feeble nod. I knew exactly what he meant.

Chapter 13

Late Sunday afternoon I was back at the office, slumped over my desk and determined to make sense of things. Further pursuit of Walter Rizzi seemed pointless. The fact that he'd changed his tune so quickly and agreed to help me was curious, but I'd already garnered more from him than I'd expected, and he'd come about as clean as he was likely to get. Conversely, I had no doubt Whitney Blue was knee-deep in this mess, but Abdiel's true identity was still the primary wildcard in a deck stacked with Jokers.

Assuming Whitney, along with this Balberith character, really were members of some murderous satanic cult, why would Jesse continue to associate with them? And if she had, due to some twisted sense of loyalty to Whitney, what investment scheme could she possibly have gotten mixed up in? Jesse had her share of faults to be sure, but poor judgment (particularly in financial matters) had never been one of them. And besides, why run? She earned a decent income in adult features. If the figure was beyond her means, why not work out a deal? Even loan sharks accepted payment plans and resorted to murder only when and if it became absolutely necessary. Can't get money from a corpse.

I lit a cigarette, leaned back in my chair and listened

to the rain. My jaw ached; I'd been clenching it apparently. Whatever Jesse had done no longer had anything to do with the money she owed. Either Balberith had come to the conclusion that he was never going to get paid, or Jesse figured that even once she came across with the vig he'd kill her anyway.

And what about Randy Wallace; had his death truly been an accident? If it wasn't, why would they murder someone who might be able to tell them where Jesse was? Kevin Niedermeyer claimed no one else had approached either of them concerning Jesse's whereabouts, and if someone had, Randy would've told him. Maybe he never got the chance...or maybe Randy's death was totally unrelated to this case and nothing more than the senseless tragedy it appeared to be.

But then, who was Abdiel? Why couldn't I find any record of him? How did he know Jesse, and why did he hire me to find her? Why did he lie about who and what he was? And why was Whitney Blue the only one who seemed to know for sure?

Initially, as Walter Rizzi had suggested, I thought Abdiel might be working with the others. If they were having trouble finding Jesse wouldn't it make sense to hire me, sit back and let me lead them straight to her? But Whitney had become terrified the moment I'd uttered Abdiel's name. If the two of them were in on this together, why would she fear him?

"She wouldn't," I said aloud.

They both wanted Jesse found, of that much I was convinced, but it had to be for different reasons. Neither Abdiel nor Whitney nor Kevin Niedermeyer had met me previously, yet they'd all known who I was from conversations they'd had with Jesse. If she still loved me, realized leaving had been a mistake and felt comfortable openly discussing our past, why hadn't she attempted reconciliation? Presuming she feared rejection on a romantic basis, Jesse still knew that if she'd come to me for help I would not have refused her.

None of it added up, and now I had to worry about this Balberith fuck, some whacked out satanic stockbroker. Then there were the freakish dreams I'd had of late—what the hell were they about? The whole scenario was preposterous, but one thing was certain. Regardless of how I approached this mystery, every road invariably led me back to one man.

Abdiel.

I checked my watch. It was just after five and already dark out. I hadn't slept in more than twenty-four hours and exhaustion had started to take its toll. Abdiel was slated to contact me the next morning, and I wanted to be coherent if and when a meeting took place. Another all-nighter was out of the question.

A sudden knock on the door startled me right out of my chair.

Knowing potential clients seldom appeared unannounced and that my social circle was virtually nonexistent did little to calm my nerves. I glanced at the desk drawer that housed my 9mm Beretta. Despite my extensive experience with firearms, the time I'd spent in combat had left me profoundly uncomfortable with them. I carried a gun only when absolutely necessary, and quickly concluded this was not one of those times. *You're tired and paranoid*, I told myself. *Chill out and answer the door.*

I looked through the peephole but the hallway light was out. Darkness stared back. "Who is it?" I called. There was no response, so I asked a second time. Again, silence. I disengaged the security chain and hesitantly reached for the doorknob.

It was ice cold against the warmth of my palm.

The window overlooking the street rattled and I spun around, half-expecting to see someone climbing through it. A burst of wind sprayed rainwater against the pane and the window rattled again. I shook my head, angry that I'd allowed an overactive imagination to get the better of me. I turned back to the door. "Anybody there?"

This time I heard movement in the hallway. As I pulled open the door the shadowy outline of someone moved from the far end of the hall toward the staircase.

"Hey! Something I can do for you?"

The figure froze and then silently reversed direction. Aware that the intruder was now facing me, I squinted at the darkness but couldn't discern any features. "Who's there?" I demanded. The shadow was now still, a vague statue just beyond my reach. "What do you want?"

"*You...*"

I curled one hand into a fist, slid the other along the wall and switched on the hallway light. An overhead fixture bathed the area in a yellow hue, transforming the phantom into an old man. He stood at the top of the stairs grinning at me, his teeth like pointed razors, eyes glistening black. It was the same man from my nightmare—the one in the church—only this time he seemed real, standing just a few feet away.

Behind him, something slithered to the floor. Snake-like, but more closely resembling a length of human intestine, as if alive, the appendage writhed about with a moist sound then slowly crept down along the stairs. My stomach lurched.

"I can feel your fear, David," his voice gurgled. "And it's *wonderful*."

A distant whisper repeated his name again and again in my mind.

The man scratched his chin with a long fingernail. "Yes," he said, answering my thoughts. "*Balberith…*"

With a dull ache throbbing through my temples, I opened my eyes and focused on a high ceiling of filthy girders and rusted steel beams. Disoriented, I rolled onto my side and realized I was sprawled out on a cold concrete floor. The light was dim, and I couldn't pinpoint its origin, but it allowed me to see a woman standing to my left.

I struggled to my feet, staggered about on legs that felt like they'd never been used and looked directly into the eyes of Whitney Blue.

She stepped closer, a crooked smile slanting her lips, and walked past me without comment. With the heels of her pumps clicking against the cement floor, I followed, mesmerized by the sway of her hips beneath a black leather skirt stretched snugly across her ass. A dank odor joined the startling chill in the air, and I began to shiver as my breath became a visible swirling mist.

I stumbled into a small room and leaned against the door frame, chest heaving. A bare light bulb suspended from the ceiling by a frayed cord provided the only light.

Whitney crawled from the shadows on hands and

knees. Nude, she began to rock her head back and forth to a rhythmic beat only she could hear, her mane of dark hair bounding about and tumbling across her shoulders. Without taking her eyes from me she slid forward, crushed her breasts against the floor and arched her back, raising her buttocks into the air.

From the darkness behind her…Balberith…his sagging, pasty bare flesh damp and matted with sweat.

He stepped closer, the inhuman tail-like appendage that moved on its own slinking from behind him and writhing about as it had on the staircase in my office building. He stood motionless as it curled upward between his legs, then plunged itself into her like a striking snake. He watched me as Whitney began to buck, slamming herself against him, forcing it deeper with each frenzied thrust.

Maniacal laughter escaped her, and as she jerked her head up, swinging her hair over and onto her back, her eyes filled with demonic glee.

"Come on," she said to me, panting between bursts of shrieking laughter. "Come on, David…*come on.*"

Balberith grabbed her hair, yanked back her head and rammed himself deeper still. Whitney continued to laugh, running her hands along her stomach. Her unicorn tattoo danced seductively with each bounce of her sweat-coated breasts, and as her body lurched, he continued his assault, fangs bared.

Whitney's eyes rolled back to white, and as her mouth fell open a horde of maggots slithered free. With each thrust from Balberith, more worm-like larva emerged, scurrying across her chin and dropping to the floor to form an undulating mass that slowly began to engulf them both.

I pushed myself back through the door and vomited at a full run. Ignoring the nausea still tearing through my abdomen, I returned to the room where I had first awakened, and searched frantically for a way out. I stopped long enough to get my bearings and realized I was in a warehouse of some sort.

A steady stream of moisture trickled onto the crown of my head.

Startled, I looked up expecting to see a leak in the ceiling but instead found myself staring into the lifeless eyes of Walter Rizzi.

He was hanging upside down like a slaughtered animal, feet tied to a beam, arms dangling loosely and a bullet wound in what remained of his right temple. Blood dripped, splashing my face, and I heard a horrifying scream, initially unaware that it was my own.

The air brakes from an eighteen-wheeler hissed at me as it stopped for a red light across the street. I blinked rain from my eyes and looked around. I was on the corner just blocks from my office, my clothes soaked and my head throbbing.

I took refuge in a doorway and lit a cigarette with shaking hands while trying desperately to remember how I'd gotten outside in the first place. Had I been sleepwalking? I assured myself none of this was real. I was stressed, dog-tired and hadn't slept in days. My mind was reacting accordingly, with an ample dose of irrational confusion and disoriented panic. Perhaps thinking and worrying about Jesse while in a state of physical and mental exhaustion had triggered something in my mind, linked me somehow to the past—and once confronted with those memories I'd reverted back to the time when

I'd originally returned from the Gulf. Either way, the terror of struggling to maintain a grip on the boundaries separating fantasy from reality was all too familiar. The doctors had warned that a recurrence of my psychological problems would forever be a possibility, and for the first time, I had begun to believe them.

Tony Barbata, an old man who had owned and operated a newsstand in the neighborhood for years, looked at me from behind a stack of magazines he was counting and waved from the next block. As I crossed the street, he smiled his nearly toothless grin.

"Shit, Dave, ain't never seen you up this early. Rough night, brother?"

I slipped beneath an awning shielding the newsstand and gave a weary shrug. "How's it going, Tony?"

The old man hacked up a ball of phlegm and spat it out on the curb. His face exhibited the usual battered features found in former fighters: a flattened nose, heavy scar tissue about the eyes and loose, leathery skin. Known as the "Portuguese Punisher" in his heyday, Tony's biggest claim to fame had been the two rounds he'd survived in a non-title bout with legendary middleweight champion Jake LaMotta back in the 1950s. Proudly displayed along the back wall of the newsstand was a faded framed photograph from the local papers which showed him collapsed on the canvas in a bloody heap beneath the headline: LAMOTTA STOPS LOCAL BOY IN TWO.

"You look wiped out, kid," he said. "What you doin' out in the rain at six in the morning?"

There was something about him that didn't seem quite right, but I couldn't put my finger on it. "Like you said," I mumbled, "rough night."

He chuckled, made a fist and pumped it at me playfully. "Found a honey? Laid a little pipe? Get as much as you can, kid, 'cause once you hit my age the shit don't work like it used to. Get all excited if I can piss a dribble out the bastard most days."

I forced a dutiful smile. "Tony, you got any Cape Cod newspapers back there?"

He stepped toward the back of the stand and rummaged through a pile of assorted papers. "Only carry a few copies, it don't sell. Got a couple used to live out that way always picks one up but—where the hell I put that fucker? Don't nobody here give a pile of rat shit about Cape Cod." He finally located the newspaper and handed it to me. "So tell me about this honey you snagged last night. She got some big ole—"

"You been reading too many of those porno rags," I said, still trying to figure out what it was about this man I had known casually for years that was on this day, askance.

He smiled again, slurped at his pink slimy gums. "Whatever you say, Davey-boy."

I looked away, quickly scanned the headlines and focused on a story in the lower right-hand corner of the front page. Fighting back shock, frustration and grief, I gripped the paper with such force it nearly tore in half.

I read the article twice.

INFAMOUS AREA BUSINESSMAN TAKES OWN LIFE.

Hyannis—Two young boys playing in an abandoned warehouse near Iyanough Road came across a grisly discovery early Sunday morning: the body of local businessman Walter A. Rizzi, 54, of Yarmouth, dead from an apparent suicide. Due to the fact that it was an unattended death, a legally mandatory autopsy will be performed, but both local and state police officials say they found no evidence to support foul play.

Unnamed sources told us Rizzi died of a self-inflicted gunshot wound to the head, and also confirmed the existence of a suicide note found on the scene.

Rizzi became known in the area for his countless legal battles with local officials, police agencies and even the public when back in the summer of 1993 he first began operating LOVESTRUCK PRODUCTIONS, an adult video production and distribution company. Despite massive local opposition, Rizzi consistently won court battles to remain in business, and although Rizzi's reputed ties to organized crime families in Massachusetts, Rhode Island and even New York dogged him for years, no proof was ever presented by any law enforcement agencies to substantiate those claims. Rizzi was quoted numerous times in response to the constant rumors, describing them as "Insulting to Italian-Americans, completely unfounded, and absolute nonsense."

Rizzi is survived by his mother, Josephine Anaro Rizzi, 76, also of Yarmouth, and a brother, Alfredo, 51, of Utica, New York.

Sara Johan-Hickey, founder and president of the Falmouth-based organization "Families for a Moral America," and one of Rizzi's most outspoken and public opponents called the incident a "tragedy, but not one unexpected. When one lives a life contemptuous of decent family values and panders to the lowest common denominator," Ms. Johan-Hickey stated from her home Sunday evening, "it is only a matter of time before your life implodes. Mr. Rizzi's fate was inevitable, but we will continue to pray for Mr. Rizzi's soul because it's the sin we hate, not the sinner—and frankly, he needs all the prayers he can get."

Several sources suggest Rizzi most likely took his life due to substantial illegal gambling debts he was rumored to have accrued but was not in a position to repay. Neither his mother nor brother was available for comment.

Funeral arrangements have not yet been released.

"Dave," Tony said, "you okay? You look like you're gonna keel over."

I returned the newspaper to him a crumpled mess, unable to speak, unable to think. As I walked away, I heard Tony chuckle, his laughter accompanied by a thick wheezing from deep within his chest. Before I'd reached the corner it had become a violent hacking cough, and it was then that I realized what was wrong about him.

Tony Barbata had died of lung cancer more than a year before.

I turned slowly, looked back. The newsstand was gone, replaced as it had been for some time now with a free-standing newspaper dispenser, the copy I'd purchased tumbling, riding the breeze into the street.

Trembling, I wandered back to my office.

Chapter 14

I don't remember crawling into bed and falling asleep, but evidently that's precisely what I did. The only memory I have is being awakened by the telephone later that morning and hearing Abdiel's suave voice on the other end of the line.

"Good morning, Mr. Drago."

"Abdiel?"

"Yes," he said with a hint of caution. "You asked that I check in with you on Monday morning. Monday morning has arrived."

I stuffed a cigarette between my lips and rummaged through the mess on my desk for a book of matches. "Yeah, right, I…"

"I'm sorry, did I wake you?"

Between the pounding in my head and the fact that my body felt like I'd been run over by a cement mixer, it didn't seem possible I'd slept at all. "Nah," I said, "it's just been a long weekend."

I let the silence on the line linger while he twisted in the wind. "Well," he eventually asked, "have you come up with anything?"

I knew that if he sensed anger in my voice I'd probably never get the chance to confront him face-to-face, so I played it cool. "Quite a bit, actually."

"Have you found her?"

"Not yet, but I'm close." I finally came across some matches, lit my cigarette and coughed out the first drag of the day. "We better get together and discuss this in person."

"Of course, yes. Where and when?"

I wanted a setting both quiet and removed from city crowds. The driving rain had once again become drizzle but there seemed no end in sight to the nasty weather and, for now, that suited my purposes. "Meet me at Buttonwood Park," I told him. "Right before the entrance on the city zoo side there's a duck pond and a bunch of benches set back from the road."

"Yes, I've been there."

The wall clock told me it was just after ten. "I'll be there in one hour," I said. "Do us both a favor and bring an umbrella."

I splashed water on my face, changed clothes and left for Buttonwood Park. Even in my car it was a short ride from the office, but I wanted to get there well before Abdiel did and scope out the area. This time I planned to have the upper hand.

As I drove through the heavy Monday morning traffic, I began to form a strategy to effectively deal with all that had taken place. My nightmares were no longer just ghoulish, disjointed flashes. The last one had actually foretold Walter Rizzi's death, and although I continued to assure myself there had to be a reasonable explanation for these events, my visions—or whatever the hell they were—had become too prophetic to ignore. For the first time I was faced with the very real possibility that what I was dealing with was something beyond the realm of intrinsic human experience, and that possibility alone was terrifying.

The problem was that I'd never put much stock in the occult or supernatural. Beyond a basic belief in God and some sort of afterlife, most of it had always struck me as childish and absurd. I'd never believed in a link between this life and the next, and after the horrors of combat, reckoned even if there was a Hell, I'd already been there. As a police officer and soldier, I'd seen more acts of cruelty and violence than most do in a lifetime, and the perpetrators were never demons, ghosts, vampires or werewolves, but alleged human beings.

Maybe this time it was different.

When I pulled into the small dirt lot overlooking the pond, but for a few ducks gliding gracefully across the water, the area was deserted. The rain and wind had blown the once brilliant orange and yellow foliage into scattered sodden piles on the ground and along gutters, and most of the trees stood bare, their branches like bony fingers reaching for a gray, dying sky.

After dark, the pond had been a favorite make-out spot for decades, and my memories of coming here with Jesse while in high school were still vivid. I closed my eyes, saw us sitting in my father's car, snuggled together and talking for hours about the lives that awaited us. Jesse describing dreams of Hollywood fame and fortune while I rambled on about one day being a policeman, both of us blissfully unaware that reality had quietly conspired to create very different destinies for us both.

I pulled on a baseball cap, stepped from the car and walked through the drizzle to the nearest park bench. The wind came in icy bursts, hushing the clamor from nearby city streets, and I found myself fantasizing that I was the last man on earth—alone, forgotten and long dead without even realizing it.

Without warning the faces of those I'd killed came to me, flickered across my mindscape like old newsreels slithering through a projector, then just as quickly dissolved, blistering as if the film had jumped off track and touched the searing heat of lighted glass.

I turned and saw Abdiel sitting on a bench that just seconds before had been vacant. He smiled at me from beneath a purple umbrella, his cashmere coat buttoned and a wool scarf wrapped tightly around his neck. "Good morning."

"Didn't see you sitting there," I mumbled.

"You appeared to be deep in thought." He motioned to the bench. "Why don't you sit down? My umbrella can easily accommodate us both."

I stood my ground.

He offered no visible change of expression. Instead, he gazed out at the pond. "Look at the ducks, aren't they marvelous creatures? Swimming along, oblivious to the rain and cold, happy as can be without a worry in the world." He laughed lightly, as if fondly recalling an old joke. "If you want proof that God exists one need look no further than nature. Only a fool would believe something so perfect, so deliberately intricate could have happened by accident." Abdiel looked at me, the smile gone. "Perfection is never accidental."

"Neither are lies."

"And yet they're often told with the hope of achieving a greater good."

"Is that what you're hoping for?" I asked. "A greater

good?”

"That and the results of your investigation to this point, yes.”

I stuffed my hands in my jacket pockets and let him think everything was fine. "Jesse got mixed up with some bad people, took the pipe on a lousy investment deal and decided to run when she couldn't pay the bill. She was in Bolton, New Hampshire a few weeks ago but by the time I found that out she was already on the move again.”

"Where did she go from there?”

"I don't know yet," I said, noticing his disappointment. "But I'll find her.”

Abdiel nodded. "Tell me about this investment deal.”

"You know anyone named Whitney Blue?”

"I've heard of her, yes. She's an old friend of Jesse's.”

He was good, an effortless liar. "Apparently Whitney introduced her to the guy who got her involved in the deal. I don't know the specifics of it, but he must be one dangerous motherfucker. The people I've spoken to all said Jesse's afraid for her life.”

"I see," he said pensively. "Who is this person?”

"Balberith.”

He never flinched. "That's an odd name.”

"I haven't been able to locate him yet," I said. "Can't find any information on him at all. I was hoping maybe you knew who he was.”

"I never heard Jesse mention anyone by that name.”

"But you know Whitney?”

"I know *of* her. We've never actually met.”

"She seemed to know who you were.”

"I'm not surprised.”

"It strikes me as strange that Jesse wouldn't have introduced her fiancée to her best friend."

"As I told you, Jesse was planning to leave the business and I assumed that once she did she'd leave people like Whitney behind as well. I saw no point in developing a relationship with the woman." Abdiel loosened his scarf. "Besides, I'd heard Whitney was involved in some peculiar things, and frankly, I didn't approve."

"Oh yeah, what sort of things?"

"Dark things…"

"Like hardcore Satanism," I said, more a statement than question.

"You spoke with her personally?"

"Of course I did."

Abdiel looked away. "And is she the one who told you about this Balberith person?"

"No."

"Then who did?"

"I'd like to tell you," I said, "but there's one small problem."

"If it's financial, I can pay—"

"Money's not the problem. You are."

"I don't understand."

"You're a liar."

He crossed his legs, feigned innocence. "I'm sure I've no idea what you're talking about, Mr. Drago."

"Don't *Mr. Drago* me, douche bag," I snapped. "Jesse was never engaged to you or anybody else. Far as I can tell she doesn't even know you."

He responded in a patient tone one might take with a befuddled toddler. "If I hadn't claimed to be Jesse's fiancée, paying such an astronomical sum of money for your services would have been suspicious. And if I hadn't agreed to pay considerably more than what you normally charge, you would've never taken the case."

"No, I wouldn't have."

"Well, there you have it." He smiled triumphantly. "I told a lie with the hope of achieving a greater good."

I stepped closer. "And now you're going to tell the truth with the hope of avoiding a greater ass-whoopin'."

Abdiel appeared wholly amused. "Are you *threatening* me?"

"Oh absolutely, yes I am."

"That's not a wise choice, Mr.—"

"No more games," I said. "I've tried running background checks on you and it's like you don't even exist. You're not Jesse's boyfriend, you don't live in Plymouth, and with the exception of Whitney nobody's ever even heard of you. The only thing I know for sure is you're a lying sack of fucking shit."

"*Please*," he said with a wave of his hand, "there's no need for such excessive profanity."

I laughed. Couldn't help it. "I'm deeply sorry if I've offended your delicate sensibilities, ass wipe, but you don't seem to fucking appreciate what I'm up against here. In three days, two people associated with this case have ended up dead. One tried to help me as best he could and the other never got the chance. I can't prove it but I know they were both murdered."

Abdiel's smile returned. "Don't forget the nightmares."

A chill that began at the nape of my neck fanned out across my shoulder blades. "I'm not asking again. Who are you?"

"I've told you, my name is Abdiel."

I unzipped my jacket and moved closer. "You're coming clean right here, right now, and you're telling me what the hell you've gotten me mixed up in, or I'll kick your balls so far up your ass you'll gag on them every time you swallow."

"Fear…anger…violence," he said with a shake of his head. "It's precisely what they want. They feed on it."

"You mean Whitney and—"

"The harlot's not the one you should be concerned with."

"Balberith, then?"

"Yes."

"If he gets to her before I do, he'll—"

"He can find Jesse whenever he wants to."

"Then why hasn't he?"

"Because he's waiting for you." Abdiel turned and looked back out at the pond. "He'll settle for Jesse but you're the one he wants."

"Why? What am I to this guy? Who is he?"

"Exactly what your recently deceased friend Walter Rizzi told you he was…*evil*."

Through a hard swallow, I asked, "And how do you figure into all this?"

"You wouldn't believe me even if I told you."

"Try me."

"Find Jesse," he replied, "and you'll have your answer."

"You're all trying to drive me crazy. That's it, isn't it? Why? Why are you doing this?" I felt my hands clench into fists. "Answer me."

When he didn't, I threw a punch at the side of his head.

Still holding the umbrella, Abdiel caught my fist with

his free hand before it could land. Effortlessly holding it frozen just inches from his temple, he sighed as if bored. I tried to break free but he tightened his vise-like grip, sending daggers of pain up into my arm as he gently lowered me onto the bench next to him. His head panned toward me, eyes blinking as if he had only just noticed me.

"Enough about all that," he said flatly. "Let's talk about you, David."

He released me and my arm flopped into my lap, lifeless and numb.

"How—how the hell did you do that?"

"David Paul Drago," he said, "born to John and Eva Drago May 12, 1963, 4:42 a.m. at Saint Luke's Hospital, New Bedford, Massachusetts. Your parents are both deceased, but you have an older sister—Natalie—presently married and living in Kansas City with her husband and three children. You speak from time to time on the telephone, usually on holidays, but haven't seen her in nearly a decade. You have two nephews and a niece, none of whom you've ever laid eyes on, and although this troubles you, since you and your sister have never been close you've learned to accept things the way they are."

I stared at him. My paralyzed arm was no longer my main concern. "You had me checked out," I said defiantly, "so what?"

He continued unfazed. "You grew up in a poor but loving home. Your parents were decent, righteous people who passed those traits to you. While other children fantasized about being sports heroes or astronauts you dreamed of only one thing: one day becoming a policeman."

I shook my head. "Common knowledge, you—"

"It was a goal you eventually obtained," Abdiel said. "You were successful for a time, until the night you and your partner responded to a call, a domestic dispute turned violent that had been phoned in by a concerned neighbor. You arrived at the tenement in time to find a woman battered and unconscious, collapsed on the kitchen floor in a pool of blood. As you and your partner frantically searched the house you heard screams from the bedroom, and when you burst through the door you saw a man in the process of raping his six-year-old daughter."

I clenched my teeth and grimaced. "Stop, you—what are you trying to prove, you—"

"At that moment you made a decision that would forever alter the course of your life."

"—sonofabitch!"

"You lost control and attacked the man," he said, ignoring me. "Your partner tried to intervene, but by the time he managed to get you away from him you'd nearly beaten the man to death. All those things you'd seen in your few short years as a policeman: the pain, horror and suffering became too much to tolerate in that one blind moment of rage. And when it was over, and that man *did* die, you and your partner planted a knife in the man's hand and claimed he'd attacked you and the beating you administered was in self-defense. You thought it was the only way to save a career you'd waited your entire life to acquire. You lied. You lied in the hope of achieving a greater good."

I looked at the ground, my vision blurred by tears, rain or both. "How do you—how do you know these things?"

"Given the fact that you'd beaten this man to death, your superiors didn't believe the story you and your partner concocted," he continued. "But they tried to protect you anyway. You and your partner held firm to your story, and there wasn't a single shred of evidence to the contrary. You were both placed on leave pending a formal investigation. And eventually, it was your partner who sold you out to save his own hide. The department, wanting to put an end to the mess, offered you a deal, and amidst rumblings of excessive force and police brutality, you were quietly given the option of resigning. If you agreed, no charges would ever be brought against you, and with your back to the wall you realized you had no other choice. You walked away a hero in the eyes of many, a disgrace in the eyes of others. But you were faced with a problem out in the real world. You could no longer be a cop, and that's all you knew how to do. The next logical choice was the military."

"*Stop*," I said again, my head spinning.

"Jesse had other plans for the two of you, and she begged you not to go. But you were too busy running from your demons to stop and listen, weren't you, David?"

"I didn't want to leave her," I heard myself say, "but I didn't know what else to do. I wanted us to get married, but she was—I—"

"You knew she'd be waiting for you once you returned."

"Yes," I said softly.

He nodded, satisfied with my response. "Everything was going along splendidly. The Army was the perfect place to hide, wasn't it? Because there you were no longer a disgraced renegade cop but just another soldier, just another spoke in the wheel. You'd managed to save some money and planned to return home and sweep Jesse off her feet. You honestly believed you could change her, make her forget those silly dreams of fame and fortune and settle for being your wife and the mother of your children. But then in the final year of your commitment the Gulf War broke out. In that ancient desert all alone and so far from home, you found yourself backed into a corner again, only this time it was literal life or death. It wasn't just a brief, one-sided skirmish for everyone, was it, David? Your demons had caught up with you after all. Do you remember that night, David? *Can* you remember it?"

"I don't...I don't want to remember..."

"Wounded and armed with only your rifle and a knife, you slipped into an enemy camp and quietly slaughtered ten men. You first killed the two on watch, and then one by one, with the cold, calculating efficiency of the machine you had allowed yourself to become, slit the throats of the others while they slept."

"Please, don't—"

"A Silver Star and a shell of the man you'd once been," he interrupted. "That's what you brought home to Jesse."

"I didn't know, I didn't—"

"Do you love her?"

"Yes." As I flexed my fingers, the feeling gradually returned to my hand and arm. "I never stopped loving her."

"Then find her."

"How?"

"Whitney Blue," he said. "She's trying to find Jesse as well. Of course, her motives are different, but if you're as smart as you pretend to be, she'll lead you right to her."

My head was still spinning, my heart racing, and for a time all I could hear was the pitter-patter of the rain as it struck the umbrella. "You know where she is, don't you."

"Yes." Abdiel exhaled slowly, and I realized that unlike my breath, his was not forming clouds as it exited his body. "But I can only help you to a certain extent. There are rules which must be obeyed, even by me."

Tears spilled across my cheeks. "Abdiel, am I dying?"

"We're all dying, David."

"Am I insane?"

"Reality is conceptual," he said. "Try to remember that."

"Am I damned? *Please*," I begged, "tell me."

After a moment he stood up and opened his free hand to reveal a deep and bloody wound in the center of his palm. "Faith," he whispered.

I scrambled to my feet, nearly fell. "This is a set-up, you fuck! Goddamn parlor tricks and smoke and mirrors—you—you want me to believe I'm insane, you—"

"'*God made Man from the beginning and left him in the hands of his own counsel. He added His commandments. He hath set water and fire before thee: stretch forth thy hand to which thou wilt. Before man is life and death, good and evil: that which he shall choose shall be given him.*' Eccleiasticus 16." He smiled and showed me his hand again.

The wound had vanished.

"That which he shall *choose* shall be given him."

Chapter 15

Frigid drops of rain tickled my eyes, and as I blinked them open, a hard-blunt object poked my ribs. "Let's go, buddy," a surly voice commanded. "Up."

I was on my side, stretched out on a park bench, just feet from the duck pond. Shivering, I wiped the water from my face and struggled into a sitting position. "What's going on?"

A policeman stood towering over me, nightstick drawn. "Christ, you reek. Have a little too much to drink last night, guy?"

I looked around. Abdiel was gone. "I don't—"

"You got any ID on you?"

I pulled my wallet from my jacket and handed him my driver's license.

"Get on your feet," he ordered. "I'm gonna have to run you in for public intoxication."

"Wait," I said, "you don't understand, I—"

"Don't give me a hard time." He slid the nightstick into his belt, reached for a pair of handcuffs with one hand and held my license up to his face with the other. "You can sleep it off in a cell for a few hours and we'll even throw in a hot meal. It's not so bad. Now stand up and put your hands—" His eyes narrowed, darted from the license to my face, then back again. "Jesus. *Dave*, is that you?"

He suddenly looked vaguely familiar. "Yeah, it…it is."

"It's me, Mike. Mike Jantos."

"Hey." I smiled, recognizing him now. We'd worked together on the force years before. "How you been, Mikey?"

He handed back my license. "A whole hell of a lot better than you, I guess. What happened? What are you doing out here, for Christ's sake?"

After a brief coughing fit, I said, "I was supposed to meet somebody."

"You better cool it with the drinking, Dave." He crouched down next to the bench for a better look at me. "Waking up on park benches ain't exactly a good sign, am I right? I know a place you can go get straightened out if that's what you need. And not for nothin', but that's what you need."

My chest burned with each breath. "I'm all right, Mikey. Really, I'm fine."

He frowned. "At least let me give you a ride home, huh?"

I looked over my shoulder, saw my Nova and his cruiser parked alongside it. "I got my car. It's all right."

"You can pick it up later."

"I'm cool, really. I can drive."

"You sure?" He stood up, watched me a while longer then gave a reluctant nod. "You're just lucky it's me that found you and not one of the newer guys. They'd run you in so fast it'd make your head spin."

We both started for our cars. "Thanks for giving me a break, man. I appreciate it."

He opened the door to his cruiser. "You all right?" he

asked. "I mean, you need a few bucks or something?"

"You're embarrassing me now."

"You'd do the same for me," he said. "I don't give a shit what they say. You were a damn good cop."

I smiled, but only because I didn't know what else to do. "No," I said softly. "I wasn't."

"That human filth got exactly what he deserved. Piece of shit had it coming, you ask me. And you know your partner—that piece of shit—he's working Internal Affairs now, go figure."

"It was a long time ago. Doesn't matter now, I..."

Mike looked away. "You take care of yourself, you hear me?"

As he drove off, I slid behind the wheel of my car, too frightened to even imagine that Abdiel had been nothing more than a dream, a shadow, a whisper in my crippled mind.

There was one other person who had seen him for sure, and only she could prove I wasn't completely insane. I lit a cigarette, started the car and headed for the Moby Cafe.

When I walked through the door, a few old men slouched in stools at the counter glanced at me with disinterest, and I saw Anna wiping off a nearby table. When she looked at me, she frowned, then quickly masked it with a smile. "Morning, Dave. How you been?"

I stayed near the entrance and let her come to me. "Anna, I need to talk to you a minute."

She tossed a rag over her shoulder and approached me cautiously. "What's up?"

"Remember when I came in here Friday?" I asked. "I met a client, he got here before I did and you sat him at a table in back. I need to know if you've seen him in here since."

"Now wait, when was this?"

"Friday morning."

"No, couldn't have been. You haven't been in here in at least a couple weeks."

I gnawed my lower lip. "Anna, you've forgotten, that's all. It was last Friday. The guy was tall, good-looking with long curly hair. He was wearing a cashmere coat, nice slacks and a heavy sweater."

"I think I'd remember him," she said with a wink. "He sounds dreamy."

"Jesus Christ, you think I'm fucking around here?"

"Hey," she said, trying to keep her voice down, "come on, Dave, watch your language, what's the matter with you?"

I took a deep breath, looked beyond her and let my eyes slowly pan the cafe. Everyone looked suspect—as if they were all straining to listen to our conversation—no one could be trusted. "Look, this is important," I said, returning my attention to Anna, "I'm talking about three days ago. Just stop and think. Please, Anna."

"You weren't here last Friday. The last time I saw you was about two weeks ago. You came in alone, sat at the counter and had a black coffee and a chocolate doughnut like always. You were in a bad mood and didn't say two words to me or anybody else."

"You're lying."

She blanched. "I'm *what*?"

I glanced around again, scanning the faces of the others

more closely this time. One old woman sat near the back dressed in black, a matching scarf covering her hair and tied beneath her chin. Her eyes looked right through me. Her face was expressionless and deeply lined, the skin like the cracked earth of a desert floor. "They got to you," I said, eyes still trained on the old woman. "They told you to say these things."

Anna moved closer, her voice barely audible. "Dave, listen to me. Please don't cause a scene in here, all right?"

The woman's dead eyes remained locked on me. Slowly, her lips curled into a devilish smile, revealing black and rotted gums.

"All I want is the truth."

"You want the truth, here it is. You look like you haven't slept in days. You need to shave, bathe, change your clothes and get some rest. Lay off the bottle too, that probably wouldn't hurt. You're a nice guy, Dave, but this job ain't exactly a dream come true, you know? It's tough enough, I don't need this shit."

I leaned against the door, knees weak. I looked over her shoulder at the old woman. Her tongue, swollen and bloody, slowly traced her cracked gray lips. "This can't be, Anna, I...I was here. You sat the guy at that table right over there, and—"

"Go home, Dave." She looked at the floor. "You're a mess. It's not even noon and you reek of booze."

The old woman's grin widened and her tongue fell from her mouth, slapping against the table with a bloody splash. Laughing now, her frail body bucking, blood poured from her mouth, coating her chin, as fingers gnarled by arthritis cupped the slab of meat from the table and held it up like some demonic sacrifice.

"Anna, you have to believe me, please, I—"

"I don't know what you're talking about. You're confused."

The old woman leaned forward, stained lips drawn together, and blew onto the tongue in her hands. It exploded into several pieces, shattering and falling about her and the others in the cafe like a black snow—like falling ash from a nearby fire.

Anna looked at the rear of the diner, obviously wondering what I had seen, then turned back to me and shook her head. "For God's sake, are you all right? What are you looking at?"

The old woman slowly stood up, blood still running from her mouth, dripping now onto the tile floor. She moved toward me, grinning, and it was then that I realized her feet were not touching the floor.

I brought my hands to my face, rubbed my eyes, ignored the quaking in my legs and did my best to restore my breathing to a normal pattern.

"Dave?" I heard Anna say. "Are you all right?"

I dropped my hands. The old woman was gone, the table where she'd been, vacant. "Please, Anna," I said, "just tell me this is all a dream."

She looked as if she might cry. "Just go home, okay? Go home and get some sleep. You're confused. You weren't here Friday. Just go home. Go home, Dave."

The last thing I saw was the look in her eyes, a horrible look that told me she was telling the truth.

I drove back to my office feeling dead inside, exactly the way I'd felt years before in the desert. Surrounded by rotting corpses, unable to tell where their blood ended and mine began, I'd watched night become day while waiting to be rescued, silently aware that my life could never be the same.

The bathroom mirror confirmed what Anna had told me. My hair was mussed and in need of washing, my eyes were bloodshot slits beneath which hung heavy black bags, and my clothes were wrinkled and soiled.

I drifted back to my desk and collapsed into the chair. I now knew what had to be done. I'd make a call to the VA hospital, talk with my doctor and arrange to have myself committed.

I opened my middle desk drawer to look for the phone book and saw the photograph of Jesse staring back at me.

The photograph Abdiel had given me.

In that split-second, the supernatural forces I was up against became a reality as tangible as the photograph in my trembling hands, and what began as nervous laughter quickly turned to uncontrollable sobs. I kissed Jesse's picture again and again, joyous and terrified at once. "I'm not crazy," I wept. "I'm not crazy. You hear me, you sonofabitch, I'm not crazy!"

But what I didn't know then, was that insanity would have been preferable to the truth.

Chapter 16

I drove across town to the YMCA, had a shower and washed my hair, shaved and changed into fresh clothes. I still wasn't going to win any beauty pageants but at least I'd lost the bleary-eyed vagrant look. Once back at the office I put a call into Father Quinn Justin, a priest I had known since childhood.

Father Justin had been a close family friend for decades. He had baptized my sister and me, given us our first communion and confirmation, and I'd even served under him as an altar boy at Saint Anne's in the city, where he had been pastor for more than twenty years. He was a beloved figure locally, known for his patience, kindness and a maniacal love of sports. A boisterous sense of humor, an ability to reach out to those less fortunate—particularly young people—and the gift of ministering without seeming pious were what always set Father Justin apart from other priests.

Instead of fire and brimstone from the pulpit, he preferred to pull up a chair and talk with a person one-on-one, and could usually be found at the neighborhood basketball courts, playing pickup games with teenagers while subtly slipping in a few Bible lessons. I had bonded with him as a child, and while I hadn't seen or spoken to him in months, I knew him to be an honest and genuinely spiritual man. If there was anyone I could go to for advice and information, it was Father Justin.

Due to his advancing age and the fact that he had suffered two heart attacks, he'd been relieved of his duties as parish pastor at Saint Anne's and assigned to a management position at a homeless shelter in the city a few months prior.

A rather plump, middle-aged black woman greeted me at the door and introduced herself as Rhonda. Her hair was tied back severely with a blue cloth scarf and her clothes consisted of worn jeans, a sweatshirt and inexpensive sneakers. She led the way through the shelter with a purposeful, almost militaristic stride, and as I tried to keep up I did my best not to stare at the countless number of people, most of who were still in various stages of sleep. I felt peculiar. I'd wandered into a bedroom, albeit a communal one, but it still deserved the same rights to privacy and respect as any other.

"Uncomfortable?" Rhonda asked without looking back.

"Little bit."

"Good," she said evenly. "Seeing human beings living like this is supposed to make you feel that way. If you weren't uncomfortable there'd be something seriously wrong with you."

We walked between two rows of metal beds that led to the foot of a large open staircase, and Rhonda climbed it with the zeal of a runner in training. I was no more than halfway up when she turned and eyed me from the top. Once I'd finally joined her there, she motioned to the sea of beds that filled the floor below us. "Mostly families," she said. "Lot of women, lot of kids."

"It's sad."

"When a puppy dies, it's sad. This here is criminal."

I figured this wasn't the time to tell her I generally liked puppies more than people, so instead, I threw her a quick, "Yes, ma'am."

"When you see people—good, honest people who just want a fair shake at life—down this low, it's hard not to let anger take the wheel, you know?"

"It must be difficult to see this kind of heartache day in and day out," I said, watching one young woman dress her toddler son. "I don't know if I could take it."

"Sometimes it doesn't seem like it, but God never gives us more than we can handle," she said. "I try to remember what Jesus said. Look into their eyes and see Him. You'll be surprised how differently you see folks."

A door behind us opened with a creak. I turned and saw a tall man in his late sixties, his silver hair combed straight back from his handsome face. Dressed in casual clothes, there was no indication that he was a priest, but there was no mistaking Father Justin's jovial smile.

"David," he said. I returned the smile and offered my hand but he gave me an engulfing bear hug instead. When he was through, he placed his hands on my shoulders and held me back for a better look. "How have you been, kiddo?"

"All right, Father. You're looking good."

He rolled his eyes. "I'm old." He glanced playfully at Rhonda. "Did she give you the five-minute lecture or the ten?"

Rhonda waved at him and smiled. "The five, the five."

"Then I saved you just in time," Justin said, motioning toward the office. "Come on in. Thanks, Ronnie."

I entered the small office. There was a desk, a phone,

two cheap plastic chairs, a file cabinet and a coffeepot. On the wall behind the desk was a small crucifix.

"Coffee?"

"Thanks." I settled into one of the chairs. "Black, please."

Justin grabbed a Styrofoam cup from the counter, filled it with steaming coffee and handed it to me. "It's so nice to see you, David. Are you still running the investigation firm?"

"I don't know that I'd call it a firm exactly, but yeah."

"You must be doing a lot of business."

"Why do you say that?"

"Haven't seen you in church in a long while," he said with a grin. "Which leaves me no choice but to assume you're incredibly busy."

"So how are you feeling?" I asked quickly.

"The ticker's not what it used to be, I'm afraid, but I'm fine, just fine." He hesitated as he rounded the side of his desk. "I take it your sister and family is doing well?"

I sipped the coffee. "Far as I know."

He eyed me suspiciously. "When's the last time you spoke with her?"

"Last Christmas."

"Shame on you, David," he said softly.

"She's out in Kansas City." I said. "You know we've never really been that close, Father. I mean, we love each other and all, but we don't have much in common. She's busy with her husband and the kids."

He nodded and slipped into his chair behind the desk. "So what's on your mind? You look troubled."

"Mind if I smoke?" I asked.

Father Justin pulled an ashtray from his desk drawer,

placed it between us and nonchalantly slid a cigarette between his lips from a pack hidden from view. "Nobody smokes anymore, David, what's wrong with you? Filthy habit, absolutely disgusting, you really should quit." He winked and lit the cigarette. "Just don't tell Rhonda."

"After two heart attacks, you probably shouldn't be—"

"Right, of course not," he said. "What was it you wanted to talk to me about?"

I quietly smoked my cigarette for a while, not sure of where to begin. "I'm working on a strange case, Father, and I was hoping maybe you could help me out with some spiritual advice."

"I can't interest you in talking sports, huh? After my beloved Red Sox went into the tank, yet again, I was genuinely looking forward to the basketball season, but it seems the Celtics have done something to anger the good Lord. Did you catch the game last night? My grandmother's got a better outside jumper than anyone on the team and she's been dead longer than you've been alive." He chuckled, then sensing my tension became more serious. "Sorry. You were saying?"

"Father, what are your views on the reality of evil?"

He arched an eyebrow. "How do you mean?"

"Well, you've always said that God's presence in our lives is as tangible as we choose to make it."

"That's right."

"Does the same go for Satan's presence?"

He took a drag, exhaled through his nose. "Hmmm. That depends, I suppose, on how one views Satan in general terms. Some biblical scholars are literalists, that is to say they believe every word in the Bible is to be taken literally, verbatim. If you follow that line of thought then certainly Satan and his influence in our lives is just as tangible as that of Christ's. Personally, I've always thought one of the most beautiful aspects of the Bible is its interpretive nature. Don't get me wrong, I believe everything within its pages is true, but it's rather clear that a great deal of the stories are purely symbolic. Remember that symbolism is one of the most effective tools one can utilize when speaking to the consciousness of the masses. Take the Apocalypse, for example. The book itself was written by Saint John the Evangelist, in Greek. He wrote it on the isle of Patmos, around 95, 96 A.D. Now, is that book symbolic of the end-times or is it meant to be taken literally? As with many books in the Bible that's open to speculation. I think the basis for all Christian belief lies in the knowledge that one day, Jesus will return, and with His return will come the end of the world as it now exists. I certainly believe Christ will come again, but I can't honestly sit here and tell you I have any idea as to how or when. The book of the Apocalypse is an outline of *possible* likelihoods, in my opinion, one of many potential futures dependent upon the course of Man and the decisions made by Man. There are those who say the signs written in the book are already coming to pass. Maybe they are, maybe they aren't. Maybe we're wrong, or maybe we're right. Maybe all the religions are. Maybe none of them are. No one can be certain, that's a matter for faith. I prefer to concern myself with what I *do* know."

"Which is?"

"That people are starving in the streets of the richest country in the world. That crime, hate and violence are rampant, and that as a people we've lost our way. I can feed the hungry, I can give them shelter and I can love them as I love Jesus. I can try to live as I would think He wants me to. That much I know for sure, and that's what I concentrate on."

I let the words sink in before asking my next question. "But what about evil specifically, Father? Can it manifest itself in human form? Can Satan send his followers here to do evil things the same as God often sends those to do good deeds?"

"Sure," he answered casually. "Again, assuming that fits into your beliefs. Regardless, there's evil all around us every day of our lives. Even the most devout atheist wouldn't argue that. Temptation exists at all times, son, and temptation, like fear and confusion, is one of Satan's most powerful tools."

"So assuming Satan is real then demons would be too, right?"

"Yes, of course."

"And if those demons exist, can they come to us in human form?"

"Theoretically they have the ability to present themselves in human form, yes, as can angels." He stood up, poured himself a cup of coffee and returned to his chair. "Remember Michael, the archangel? Many Christians believe that he's the angel of death and that he often comes to Earth disguised as a human wanderer. Sort of like Cain. He became a nomad after killing his brother Abel in the book of Genesis, similar idea."

"So following that train of thought," I said, "if God can send angels—"

"Satan can send his as well," he interrupted. "Listen, David, just what kind of case are you involved in?"

I took a deep breath. "I've come across some people I

believe to be hardcore Satanists," I said. "I'm trying to figure out exactly what their belief system is."

"'*Up is down, pleasure is pain, darkness is light, slavery is freedom, madness is sanity,*'" he said. "That's a basic credo of their religion."

I sipped my coffee. "But are these sorts of people just a bunch of nuts or are they dealing in reality?"

"Depends on the individual, I suppose. There are many Satanists and satanic groups and churches that don't even believe in Satan as a literal being. But for the hardcore crowd he's as real to them as our beliefs are in Christ," he said. "It just depends what side of the fence you're sitting on. Of course there are those who think we're all a bunch of lunatics and that religion in any form is little more than a security blanket, fairy tales we convince ourselves are real to help us get through life. Personally, I feel sorry for people like that. Doesn't mean they're wrong though. For me, deep down, I think every human being knows there's a God, some greater con-sciousness."

"And a Devil?"

"Could be."

I crushed my cigarette in the ashtray and sat back. "Father, have you ever heard the name *Abdiel*?"

He paused in thought for a moment. "Yes."

It took everything I had to prevent my mouth from dropping open. "*Yes*?"

"You weren't paying attention in school," he said with a smile. "John Milton's *Paradise Lost* ringing any bells?"

"Vaguely, yeah, I—I mean I know what it is, I read it a million years ago in school but—"

"Well, before the war in Heaven, Satan was a high-ranking angel with several other angels under his command. When the war began, Abdiel was the only one of his subordinates who refused to rebel against God. Satan made himself a throne in Heaven, which of course was blasphemous, and set about convincing the others to follow him once the rebellion began. Speaking to all the angels under him, Satan told them they were fools to obey God, and that they were meant to rule instead of being servants to the Lord. Abdiel, however, taunted Satan and said that rebelling against their creator was madness. It was Abdiel's contention that since God had created all of the angels—including Satan—he was obviously superior and stronger than they were. Abdiel left his former comrades behind to be manipulated and tricked into what turned out to be an enormous error. Some people believe that God rewarded Abdiel for his loyalty and often sends him to Earth to help those who find themselves in similar situations where Satan is attempting to trick them into rebelling against God."

As I felt the blood drain from my face, I asked, "And what about Balberith? Ever heard of him?"

"There's a name you don't hear very often. Balberith is supposedly Hell's secretary and archivist. In mythology he is believed to be the one who notarizes deals between Satan and Man. Sort of an executive assistant or office manager in Hades." He chuckled. "I hope you're not about to tell me you've met either one of them."

"No, no," I said through forced laughter. "I just came across those names in the course of my investigation and wondered who they were."

"Can you give me any specifics about the case?"

Although I didn't want to lie to the man, I didn't have

much choice at that point. "Basic missing person thing," I said. "A teenage girl got mixed up with a cult and took off."

Justin shook his head. "Have you been able to locate this poor child?"

"Not yet." I put my coffee aside. "Father, you said Balberith notarizes deals between Satan and man—"

"In mythology," he interjected.

"Right, in mythology. But could such a concept actually exist?"

He butted his cigarette, returned the ashtray to its hiding place and fanned the lingering smoke away with his hands. "You mean can man truly make deals with Satan? Sell their souls to him in exchange for worldly riches and such?"

"Yes."

"Do you want the company line or my own personal opinion?"

"The latter."

"Publicly the church has never officially admitted that Satan even exists, but I can tell you that nearly every diocese has a priest who performs exorcisms. Few of us ever know who they are, and it's my understanding that these priests execute their duties in parishes far from their home base. In other words, a priest from California might perform an exorcism here in New England where no one knows who he is. He's brought in quietly, does what he can and goes home. If there wasn't a very real and devastating evil force running loose on this planet, why would there be a need for exorcists? Now, can that evil force be defined as a red devil with horns and a pitchfork? Who knows? Most people believe possession is simply mental illness or hysteria, and it very well may be. But whatever form it takes, wouldn't it seem logical that if God can enter your heart, give you a spiritual awakening and change your life for the better, then Satan could probably do just the opposite? Taking it a step further, the Devil can't get his hands on you unless you allow him to, and who in their right mind would want that? As a result, Satan must trick people into coming over to his side by offering success or some similar promise. Thus, the traditional deal with the Devil where a mortal sells his or her soul. Unfortunately, his promises are empty and fleeting. Jesus tells us to live for the next world—not this one—and as Christians we know we're protected from the forces of evil through our faith in God. Faith, essentially, is our last line of defense. If you're the type of person who needs every last mystery explained and proven in tangible human terms, you're in trouble. Faith, that's the key."

I nodded absently. "That's exactly what he said."

"What who said?"

I recovered quickly and smiled. "Jesus."

"Oh. Yes, right."

"Father, if someone did make a deal with the Devil for whatever reason," I asked, "would there be any way to break it?"

Justin's expression grew dark. "What are we really talking about here?"

"What if this girl I'm trying to find sold her soul when she joined the cult," I said carefully. "Could she still be saved?"

"Do you honestly believe that's a possibility, that she did such a thing?"

"I'm not sure it is possible, that's what I'm asking." I looked at the floor. "I don't know what to believe at this point, Father."

He rose from his chair, crossed the room and tossed his cup into a wastebasket. "Regardless of Satan's power, God's is always greater. Any sin can be forgiven—even one of that magnitude—but only if the person repents and asks God's forgiveness. If the person is truly sorry and honestly seeks redemption, Jesus *will* forgive them."

"And short of that?" I asked.

"Short of that, the person had better be fond of eternal damnation." He folded his arms across his chest. "Eternity's a long stretch, David. Even longer than the last time the Sox won the World Series, and trust me on this, that's a long damn time."

I nodded and gave a brief smile. "Thanks, Father. You've been a big help."

"I'm always here." He moved closer and placed a hand on my shoulder. "Are you sure this case is the only thing bothering you?"

"Yeah," I said, standing. "I'm okay."

"You know," he said softly, "I never really had the chance to tell you how proud I was of you after that horrible business in Iraq."

I looked into his eyes. "Why would you be proud of me?"

"I spend two days a month at a VA hospital in Boston. A lot of those boys never walk out of those places." He smiled warmly. "After all you'd been through, I was happy to hear you'd pulled through, gotten your head together."

"There but by the grace of God go I."

"Amen." He gave me a firm pat on the back. "Don't be a stranger, David. You're a good kid, lighten up on yourself. Remember there's plenty of pain in this world but not a hint of it in the next. When you get there, I'll be waiting, and I plan to be the first one to say I told you so."

I prayed he was right, but something told me this would be the last time I'd ever see Father Justin.

In this life, or the next.

Chapter 17

Nightfall found me at a convenience store spending some more of Abdiel's money. I bought something that claimed to be a sandwich, a thermos of coffee, a losing lottery ticket and two packs of Camels, then using the original address Walter Rizzi had given me, headed out to see what Whitney Blue was up to.

I rented a car from the usual spot. The drive to Boston was uneventful.

I found her building on Marlborough Street—a quaint, quiet, tree-lined street of brownstones in Boston's Back Bay—parked in a space a few doors down and settled in. The lights were on in her second-floor apartment but I didn't see any activity or signs of life.

Since it was Monday night, I figured her nightclub was either closed or didn't generate enough business to warrant her presence. My only hope was that she had other plans.

By ten o'clock that hope was dwindling. I'd been sitting in the car for more than four hours, and although the rain had died down it was still damp and cold out. The last thing I needed was a dead battery, so I used the car heater in brief intervals, bundled up in an old blanket I'd brought with me and tossed in the back seat, and did my best to stay awake.

A few minutes before midnight Whitney emerged from the brownstone in a long black coat and matching beret then hurried across the street and slipped behind the wheel of her Volvo.

As she drove toward the top of the block I started the car. She turned the corner and I followed, keeping a few car-lengths of distance between us. She made her way toward Massachusetts Avenue, turned on Boylston, continued into the theater district and eventually reached the bright lights of Chinatown. When she pulled over and parked in front of a restaurant, I circled the block and found a space a safe distance behind her.

I'd lucked out. The entire front wall of the restaurant was glass. It was a cafeteria-style joint with small tables scattered throughout and a row of booths to the right of the entrance. I watched Whitney saunter over to a booth and slide in across from a rotund, middle-aged man dressed in a cheap suit several sizes too small and a severely wrinkled raincoat. He stuffed his bloated face with a mouthful of noodles, gave a friendly nod and wiped his hands with a napkin.

Whitney was subdued, her expression unemotional, but as their conversation continued the fat man became more animated, talked with his hands and continually looked around nervously, as if expecting someone else to join them unannounced.

They concluded their discussion roughly fifteen minutes later then left the restaurant together. Once outside, they spoke briefly before Whitney returned to her car and drove off, leaving the man standing on the curb with a troubled expression.

Between her home and work addresses, I could find

Whitney basically whenever I wanted to, but I knew I might not get another crack at this newest player and decided to tail him instead.

He waddled across the street, coming within a few feet of my car. Once he'd crossed to the next block I locked the car and followed on foot.

We ended up two streets over in the middle of the Combat Zone. The neighborhood consisted of an adult book and video store, two seedy strip clubs, a dilapidated hotel and a liquor store with iron bars over the windows. The streets, teeming with hookers, an array of sleazy characters and several homeless people, were shrouded in darkness but for the occasional neon sign or flashing light. The man stopped and spoke briefly with a weary prostitute he seemed to know, then ambled across a garbage-strewn alley and disappeared inside a three-story building just beyond the last club.

I stood on the corner and sized up the hooker. In her middle to late twenties, with bad skin and an even worse dye-job, she bore the hollow features and rail-thin body of a heroin addict. She wore a waist-length imitation suede jacket, a miniskirt, stiletto heels and looked like she was gradually freezing to death. Within the span of five minutes, she checked her watch seven times and kept glancing at the building the fat man had entered. Assuming they'd made an appointment, I casually walked across the street to the front steps and slipped through the front door.

With a plan still forming in my mind, I peered through the darkness of a cramped entryway. There was a staircase directly in front of me and a row of mail slots on the wall to my right. The first two were unmarked, but the third had a piece of masking tape above it on which the name *Watson* had been written with a magic marker.

I moved into the shadows just beyond the front door and leaned against the wall. A small but plump rat appeared from nowhere, scampered between my feet and disappeared into a portal previously gnawed in the wall. Before I had a chance to react, the door swung open and the prostitute staggered in.

"Jesus," she mumbled, "he ain't never gonna replace that fucking light bulb."

I came up behind her, wrapped one hand around her waist and covered her mouth with the other. I pulled her back against me. "Don't make a sound," I whispered. "Just do what I say and I won't hurt you, understand?" When she didn't nod or respond I tightened my grip. "*Understand?*"

She bobbed her head and let out a quiet whimper.

"I'm gonna take my hand away," I told her. "You scream and I'll snap your neck."

When I released her she stood perfectly still. In a hushed voice she said, "I got a pimp that'll fuck you up if you don't leave me alone, motherfucker."

"Yeah, whatever." I put a hand on her shoulder and turned her around. "Who's the fat guy?"

"You a cop?"

"I ask, you answer. Let's try again. Who is he?"

"You mean Earl?" She wiped her nose with the back of her jacket sleeve and shivered. "He's a steady customer."

"He lives here?" I asked.

"He's got an office on the third floor."

"What kind of office?"

She shrugged. "Small one."

"No," I shook my head, "Christ, give me strength. What does he do for a living?"

"Oh. He's a detective."

"A cop?"

"No, private."

I hadn't been expecting that answer, and it took me a moment to collect my thoughts. "Does he work with anybody or is he alone up there?"

"He's alone."

"And expecting you, right?" She nodded. "Does he carry a piece or have any weapons in the office you know about?" When she hesitated I took her chin in my hand and raised her head until our eyes met. "What's your name?"

"Royce. You know, like Rolls Royce."

"Cute. Don't fuck with me, Royce. Does he have any weapons?"

"He keeps a .38 in his desk," she said softly.

"And how do you know that?"

Her eyes darted between the floor and mine. "He… sometimes he likes to, you know, do stuff to me with it."

I pulled a wad of cash from my pocket, peeled off a hundred bucks in twenties and handed them to her.

"What I got to do for this?"

"Just take the night off, okay?"

She counted the money, then looked at me. "That's it?"

"And forget you ever met me."

"It's forgot." She stuffed the money into her jacket pocket and smiled at me. "You want to know anything else?"

"Yeah, how long it'll take you to get the hell out of

here." Once she was gone, I slowly started up the stairs, careful not to trip in the darkness, and eventually found Watson's office at the end of a hallway on the third floor. The rest of the building was unoccupied and deathly quiet, but as I neared the door I could hear water running. I listened for a moment, then knocked lightly.

"Come on in, babe," a raspy voice said. "It's open."

I stepped inside and saw Watson with his back to me, standing over a sink and washing his hands in a small bathroom to my left. He'd removed his raincoat and suit jacket but still sported a faded dress shirt and a pair of slacks stretched to the near breaking point across his enormous ass.

I glanced around and saw a shopworn couch, two chest-high file cabinets against the back wall and a desk blanketed in paperwork, empty doughnut boxes and a mug of aged coffee with soggy cigarette butts floating in it. A grimy overhead fixture cast the room in an odd brown tint, and a stale scent permeated the air.

"Go ahead and get naked," Watson suggested. "I want to wear the panties this time."

Sweet Jesus, I thought, *even if that's possible, that's not something I ever want to see.*

"Get the strap-on out of the file cabinet," he said. "I think it's in the second drawer on the right."

Whatever he was paying Royce, it wasn't enough. I moved quietly across the room, leaned against the front of his desk and waited.

"You hear me, bitch?" He shut the water off. "I said, you *hear* me, bitch?"

Watson stepped out of the bathroom with a mischievous smile. The second he saw me, it was gone.

"Now just who are you calling a bitch?" I said.

"Shit, who—who the hell are you?"

"Your new strap-on buddy, apparently."

His face turned a deep crimson. "What are you doing in here? Where's Royce?"

"She can't make it tonight."

He put his hands on his hips and released a defeated sigh. "What do you want?"

"We need to talk."

"About what?"

"I think you know," I said. "I'm David Drago."

"If you don't clear out of here, I'm gonna—"

"I know this is a stretch but try to be smart. Your name's Earl Watson, you're a private detective and you're working for Whitney Blue. I'm not leaving until I know why."

He scratched his salt and pepper hair, but only to distract me from the change in his dark, piggish eyes. "I got no idea what you're talking about."

"I need some answers," I told him, "and I don't give a shit how I get them, you with me? We can do this easy or hard, it's your call."

Without response, he lumbered toward me with surprising speed for a man his size. I waited until he was close enough then kicked out the side of his knee with the heel of my boot. Watson squealed and went down like a charging rhino hit with a hunter's kill shot, clutching his damaged knee and rolling around on the floor.

I squatted next to him. "You okay, Earl?"

"Fuck you," he spat. "My knee, it—Christ, my knee—you fuck—my *knee!*"

I grabbed him by the shirt collar, pulled him up into a

sitting position then backed away and waited while he struggled to his feet. He limped to his desk chair and carefully lowered himself into it, his gut heaving as a thin line of perspiration broke out across his forehead. "I...I think I'm having a heart attack."

"Then we better hurry." I moved around the side of the desk and sat on the corner closest to him. "I know you met with Whitney earlier tonight. What were you hired to do?"

Earl rubbed his knee with both hands and shot me a dirty look as his breathing rate slowly returned to normal. "You're fucking with the wrong guy, Drago. I know all about you, and there ain't a damn thing you can do to stop this."

"To stop what, Earl?"

"Go fuck yourself."

An eerie chill came over me, as if the blood running through my veins had turned to ice water. "I'm not normally a violent guy, but I've got to warn you, I'm feeling real Old Testament tonight. You should appreciate that, Earl."

He lunged for his middle desk drawer but I stepped forward and swung the point of my elbow around into his mouth. With a loud grunt, he brought his hands to his face in an attempt to stop a sudden spray of blood, leaned over his desk and spit out two teeth that had snapped off at the gum line.

Earl's eyes filled with tears, and I thought he might lose consciousness. Instead, he gagged, coughed out another mouthful of blood and looked up at me helplessly.

I reached into the drawer, pulled out the .38 and put it in my jacket pocket. "Come on, you're all right, shake it off. Just a couple Chicklets, you'll be fine."

A long string of blood and drool hung from his bottom lip as he applied pressure in an attempt to stop the flow of blood. "*Oo bwote ot two ah mah fuh-in teef!*" he cried. "*Oo mah-ah-fuh-ah, mah teef! Ma fuh-in teef!*"

I went into the bathroom, yanked a roll of toilet paper from the dispenser and fired it at him. "Clean yourself up, Buckwheat."

Earl frantically pressed a wad of paper against his mouth and continued to stare at me in disbelief. I knew he was in considerable pain, and I actually felt sorry for the poor bastard, but the look in his eyes left no doubt that he was ready to cooperate. "Now," I said evenly, "how do you know Whitney?"

"*Tee a owe fwen.*"

"An old friend?" I waited to continue until he'd nodded in the affirmative. "What did she hire you to do?"

"*Fine tum bwoad.*"

I resumed my position on the corner of the desk and reached for my cigarettes. He flinched but relaxed once he realized I wasn't going to hit him again. "Jesse Greenlaw?"

He tossed aside the blood-drenched toilet paper, quickly replaced it with a fresh handful and leaned back in his chair. "*Yeth, Dethee Gweenwa,*" he moaned. "*I gah-ah go to ah hop-eh-toe now.*"

"Don't be a pussy, Earl." I lighted my cigarette and exhaled a cloud of smoke in his face. "You come up with anything yet?"

"*Yeth.*" He pulled the paper from his mouth to see if the bleeding had stopped. It hadn't, but he seemed to be getting better at forming actual words. "I found her."

Time seemed to freeze at that exact second. "What?"

"You heard me."

"How'd a piece of shit like you find her before I did?"

"*Geth* I'm better than you."

"That can't be it." I dropped the cigarette with no regard for the floor and stepped on it. "Where is she?"

He smiled through the pain and spit out more blood. "No way."

I leaned closer. "Earl, listen to me very careful. I will beat your ass to a pulp right in that fucking chair. You'll be pissing blood and eating your meals through tubes for a month of Sundays."

The smile dissipated, and his beady eyes scanned the room in a futile attempt to find an avenue of escape. The blood from his torn gums had slowed, and he dabbed at them with some fresh toilet paper.

"I used to be a cop," he said, his tone distant, removed, "same as you. I got a connection at the registry of motor vehicles, had her run the plate on Jesse's Mercedes. A couple days ago it came up stolen in Worcester. Cops pulled over some young guy driving it. Kid had a record a mile long—mostly car theft—and was looking at doing time since he had so many priors. From what I could find out the kid claimed a woman sold it to him for five hundred in cash. He was on his way to sell it to a chop shop when they picked him up. His description of the woman matched the owner of the vehicle, Jessica Greenlaw, but the cops didn't buy the kid's story. Since no reports had been filed, they figured he'd jacked the car and probably killed her in the process. They haven't been able to locate Jesse, so right now this kid's rotting in a cell waiting for a hearing while the D.A.'s office tries to find her."

"Great," I said. "Now the cops are involved."

He nodded. "Which don't leave any of us much time, see?"

"What's that mean?"

"Whitney's got to find Jesse before the cops do," he said. "That's what it fucking means. She's trying to make points with—"

"—Balberith?"

His expression failed to conceal his surprise, but he recovered quickly and registered a contemptuous smile. "Who?"

I took my lighter, flicked it and held the flame close to his face. "Where is she?"

Earl licked the flame, lapping at it and giggling as he widened his smile to expose bloody gums.

I tossed the lighter aside, grabbed him by the shirt with both hands and jerked him toward me. "Where is she, you motherfucker!"

He began to laugh, his considerable girth jiggling in my grasp. "You can't stop it, Drago. You can't—"

"Where!"

"It took me two days of canvassing the neighborhood where she sold the car before I finally found her," he told me. "Jesse was hiding out in a fleabag motel in Worcester. I was just about to put a call into Whitney when she checked out. I followed her to the bus station and watched her get on a bus to Cape Cod."

"She's still in Massachusetts?" I asked. "Why would she come back here?"

"Maybe she's hiding in plain sight," he said. "This time of year, the cape's deserted, and besides, I'm sure Jesse figures we think she's on the other side of the country by now. But she knows she can't run forever, Drago.

She took the deal and now Balberith wants what's his."

"Where'd she end up?"

"Fuck you."

"Fuck *me*?" I shook him like a nanny. "Fuck *me*?"

"I can't tell you, all right?"

As I tried to pull him to his feet, his shirt tore under the tremendous weight and he collapsed back into the chair. Hanging from a chain and dangling between his fleshy breasts were a five-pointed star and an inverted crucifix, side by side. I backed away, grabbed the .38 from my pocket and pointed it at him.

"Her soul belongs to our Lord, asshole." Earl stood up and limped closer. "You should've been there the night Whitney summoned him. Most amazing thing I've ever seen in my—"

"Sit down." I motioned to his chair with the .38.

"It was years ago," he said, eyes ablaze, "but I'll never forget it. It was the greatest night of my life, Drago. Jesse was the one who wanted the deal. She asked Whitney to make it reality and—in Lucifer's name—she did. I could hardly believe it myself. I'd always known Whitney was powerful, but—"

I rushed him, pushed the gun under his chin and pinned him against the wall. "I don't know what kind of scam you people are pulling or how you got inside my head, but just because a couple of nuts decide to join a cult and name themselves after mythological characters and—"

"There were dark prayers recited," he said excitedly, "a Black Mass was performed. A child was abducted, sacrificed, and I watched Whitney remove his heart, offer it up and eat it like a rabid dog."

My legs felt weak as doubt and denial became fear more savage and engulfing than I had ever before experienced. "I want the truth," I said, jamming the .38 against his temple. "Not some bullshit horror story!"

A whispering chant emanated from his bloody lips as his eyes rolled back in his head. I slapped him around until he returned from whatever dark place he had escaped to. "That *is* the truth," he finally said. "The greatest feat Satan ever performed was convincing the world that he was only a myth. He's not, Drago, he's not. I know. I've seen him, I—I've felt his power and his presence."

"Who is Abdiel?" I asked. "How does he fit into this?"

"He's the enemy," Watson said softly.

"Your enemy or mine?"

"Time will tell."

I raised the .38 as if to strike him with it, then thought better of it and returned the barrel to his temple. "If you expect me to believe there are angels and demons waging some sort of battle for Jesse's soul, you picked the wrong mark, Watson. I know I'm not crazy, goddamn it. I know—"

"Keep talkin'," he said with a smile. "Keep telling yourself that. None of it matters. Don't you get it? Whitney pulled it off. She did what had to be done and brought Balberith here. Once the child died, its blood was poured into a goblet and we all drank from it. We made the evil real."

I forced myself to ask a question I wasn't sure I wanted the answer to. "You're telling me Jesse was there when all this happened?"

"Of course not, she was brought in after the fact, once Balberith joined us on behalf of our master." He again began to laugh. "We couldn't know for sure if it would work, but when he appeared in all his glory there was no doubt, Drago, no doubt that Whitney had been right. We didn't have to waste our time with faith anymore because he was standing right there in front of us, as real as you or me. And if Balberith existed, then surely our dark father must. I cried that night. Dropped to my knees and cried like a baby because I knew then that I was part of something bigger and more powerful than any of us."

"Where did this take place?"

"Whitney's apartment," he said. "Jesse made the deal with Balberith. Her soul in exchange for…"

"For what? In exchange for *what*?"

"Ask her yourself."

"Riches, fame—what?"

The tension in his body slackened. "When I told Whitney, I'd found her, she said you'd come. She said it was my time for sacrifice. I can't tell you anything else. The rest has to come from Whitney herself."

I cocked the hammer on the .38 and increased the pressure on his temple. "I'll blow your fucking head off, Watson."

"I know," he giggled. "I know."

"You're insane."

"Pleasure is pain."

My reflection in the bathroom mirror was startling. The blood spattered across my face and neck had already started to darken and congeal, and my eyes had assumed a glazed, vacant stare.

With my ears ringing, I pulled the cleanest towel I could find from the rack, ran the water and washed up. Once finished I zipped my jacket closed to conceal the stains on my shirt, and returned to the main room.

Watson was collapsed near the wall in a growing pool of blood mixed with brain tissue and skull fragments, the back of his head gone and that same demonic grin on his face.

Chapter 18

I took the dead man's trench coat from a hook on the wall and slipped it on. It was several sizes too big and had a peculiar smell but effectively masked the traces of blood along the front of my leather jacket. The .38 was on the corner of his desk and still warm. I hid it in one of my pockets, made a quick inspection of the office and tried to remember what I'd touched. Using the sleeve of the coat I wiped the doorknob clean then shut off the lights and returned to the hallway, quietly closing the door behind me.

As I descended the steps, I still felt numb and cold inside. Why I killed Earl Watson I really couldn't say. I had no memory of pulling the trigger, only flashes of blood and the deafening discharge of the .38 echoing in my mind.

I ignored the urge to run, stepped through the front door of the building and walked across the street. It seemed impossible the people milling about the neighborhood hadn't heard the shot, but the sound of gunfire in that part of town after dark wasn't unusual, and no one seemed the least bit interested.

Avoiding eye contact with anyone, I kept my head down until I'd reached the next block and had left most of the Combat Zone in my wake. I ducked into a doorway, long enough to light a cigarette, and then headed back to my car.

On the corner, hands on her hips and a knowing smile on her face, stood Royce. Our eyes remained locked until she turned and strolled off in the opposite direction of my car. She hesitated at the curb, looked over her shoulder at me and continued on her way. No words were spoken, but I was inexplicably drawn to her. Her eyes told me to follow, and I felt I had no choice but to comply.

Keeping several feet between us I trailed her through two blocks of the theater district until she reached the Park Plaza Hotel. Across the street, she stopped at the entrance to the subway, looked back at me again and disappeared down the steps.

By the time I reached the stairs, she was out of sight. Despite the cool air, the aroma of urine and other lurid smells wafted up to street level, but I forced myself after her still. The staircase emptied into a short hallway, the walls covered in rows of filthy square tiles and the cement floor sticky and soiled. I jogged by an unmanned token booth, jumped a set of turnstiles and looked both ways.

The platform was empty. Overhead fluorescent lights illuminated the beginning of the tunnel but beyond their reach dwelled only darkness. I could hear the rumbling of a distant train and the sound of water trickling as it leaked down from the streets above.

I walked closer to the tunnel, the heels of my boots clicking against pavement and the weight of the gun in my coat pocket a constant reminder of its continued lethal presence. I took a long pull on the cigarette, tossed it aside and saw the tunnel lights blink just before a train rounded the bend and slid into view. Metal wheels screeched against the rails as it came to a gradual stop, and the doors opened in unison.

The car appeared empty.

I moved closer, leaned forward and looked beyond the doors. A lone man in torn, soiled clothes was stretched out on one of the benches, an old newspaper covering him like a blanket. His feet were wrapped in old plastic garbage bags secured with what looked like duct tape. As I focused on them, they moved, and the man slowly pushed himself up into a sitting position.

The newspaper fell away, floated gracefully to the floor and revealed the man's face. Covered with boils and rotting flesh, he smiled, splitting the skin on his cheeks as he did so.

I jumped back and fumbled for the .38 just as the doors slid shut. The train jerked forward and slithered into the tunnel, the demon's face pressed against the window, eyes watching me until the train was absorbed into darkness.

A giggle arose from the pitch-black just beyond the platform. I drew the .38, spun to my right and saw Royce staring up at me from the tracks. Before I could speak, she retreated into shadow.

Despite a sudden shortness of breath, I chased after her, climbed down a small steel ladder at the edge of the platform and dropped down near the tracks. The tunnel was as quiet as a tomb, and but for the faint glow of occasional low-watt bulbs mounted near the ceiling, just as dark.

With the gun still leveled in front of me and my heart audibly thudding against my chest, I continued forward, careful to stay clear of the rails. Visibility was horrible but sufficient enough to reveal a herd of startled rats scattering from view a few feet away.

I took each step as if expecting the ground to cave in at any moment, then stopped as a series of strange sounds seeped from the surrounding darkness.

Whispers swirled around me, grew louder then faded just as quickly. I glanced behind me, saw only the dimly lit platform, turned around and looked directly into the eyes of Balberith. "Jesus Christ!"

"Not even close."

I locked my arms and trained the .38 at his forehead. "Don't—don't you fucking move."

The old man's face showed no expression whatsoever. He opened his mouth and slowly ran his tongue along the pointed edge of his teeth. "How does it feel to be knocking at the Devil's door, David?"

"I already killed one man tonight," I said, chest heaving. "I won't think twice about making it two."

Balberith glanced at the slimy, filthy walls as if seeing them for the first time. "You killed ten men," he reminded me. "Watson makes eleven."

"Where's Jesse?"

"Just beyond your reach." His black, feline-like eyes blinked slowly. "Come with me and we can end all of this here and now. It's you I want."

I forced a swallow, tried to hold the gun steady. "Why? Why me?"

The ground trembled, the tunnel vibrated and the light bulbs rattled overhead, clacking against the tiled walls as a burst of foul air blew past. "Your soul is more valuable to me," Balberith said. "Darker, stained with death."

"Tell me where Jesse is."

Water dripped from the ceiling, splashed his head. Something small and insect-like crept quickly beneath his flesh, as if scurrying from the moisture. He reached for me with open hands, the nails on his fingers more closely resembling talons. "Come with me and I can set you free."

The vibration became stronger as another train drew closer. I stepped back, saw ghostlike lights slinking along the wall and realized I'd never make it back to the platform in time. "We'll both die down here if you don't tell me where she is."

Small flames flickered, reflected in his eyes as if he were staring directly into a fire. I'd seen this before, but couldn't remember where. "Don't you see?" he said with a smile. "That's exactly what I want."

I threw myself against the wall, pressed my back into it as hard as I could as the train rounded the corner and rushed toward us. Balberith made no attempt to move, standing with arms outstretched in mock welcome.

"Take my hand, David. Take my hand."

I braced myself, slammed shut my eyes and let out a primal, defiant scream. As the train sped past with a loud roar, I forced my eyes open to see a blur of cars rushing by just feet from my face. The interior lights blinked off then on, the passengers inside obscure flashes swept off into the black depths of the tunnel.

Amazed and grateful to be alive, I staggered from the wall, nearly fell, and instantly recoiled.

Balberith was gone.

Lying across the tracks in his place were Royce's mangled remains.

Chapter 19

I drove through Boston as if in a trance—only vaguely aware of what I was doing—and parked at the corner a block from Whitney's apartment, leaving myself the option of a quick escape onto Mass Avenue. As I hoofed it back down Marlborough Street through the rain, I saw that the lights in her apartment were off and her car was nowhere to be seen. Wherever she'd gone I could only hope she stayed there a while.

As expected, the front entrance to the building was rigged with a security buzzer. I slipped around back into an alley, sized up the fire escape and after several failed attempts managed to jump high enough to grab hold of the metal ladder. It slid free and stopped just inches from the ground. I waited to make sure the building remained dark, then quietly climbed up to the first platform. The temperature had warmed a bit, and the rain was gradually turning to a wet, slushy snow. I pulled the .38 from my pocket and ascended the steps to the second-floor fire escape at the rear of Whitney's apartment, then scaled the railing and hopped down onto the platform just inches from a double set of windows. Thick dark curtains blocked the view, and I noticed two hanging plants above my head, both withered and dead in the cold.

I checked the windows for sensors, wire or any other

traces of a trip alarm. They were clean. The locks on both windows were engaged, the mechanisms standard turn-bolts but impossible to open without first breaking the glass. I crouched down, wrapped my hand in coat sleeve and waited for a particularly strong and noisy gust of wind before punching out a small section of the top pane.

I pushed the curtain open, reached blindly through the jagged hole and unlocked the window. It opened easily, and I crawled through, my feet crunching glass as I dropped down into a large kitchen.

Although the only light came from a small bulb under the hood of a stove, it allowed me to make out the rest of the room and a doorway with a large living room beyond. Once my eyes had focused, I crept past an island counter surrounded by tall stools and above which hung several pots, pans and assorted cooking paraphernalia. The kitchen reminded me of a fancy model one might see in an appliance store: spotless, pristine and equipped with every modern convenience, yet void of any personal touches whatsoever. The table had even been set with a rose-colored candle encased in glass at the center and four place-settings of china complete with water and wine goblets.

I breathed through my mouth and listened to what the apartment had to say.

The lone intrusion to the silence was the steady hum of a refrigerator. Satisfied that I was alone, I returned the .38 to my pocket and crossed into the living room.

A large-screen television, speakers and a stereo system bookended by matching oak cabinets stocked with videotapes, CDs and hardcover books filled an entire wall.

The hardwood floors shone even in the darkness, a modern but conservative couch and matching chairs filled out the room, and three windows fitted with lacy white curtains suggested that in the light of day the area was bright and cozy. I'm not sure what I'd expected to find, but this certainly wasn't it.

I quickly inspected the contents of the cabinets and found an extensive library of classic films mixed with a few current titles, CDs ranging from dance music to jazz, and various best-selling novels along with an occasional celebrity biography. But nothing to indicate that Whitney was involved in the adult film business or the black arts. Even the prints on the walls were nondescript, modestly priced and typical of the art found in most homes.

Two fashion magazines and a *TV Guide* were stacked neatly on a glass coffee table alongside an extravagant remote control, and a small bar beneath a mirror occupied the opposite wall.

I noticed the front door at the end of a small foyer, but turned and instead followed another hallway that led to the rest of the apartment.

The first door housed the bathroom, so I continued on until I found the master bedroom. From the canopy bed to the mirrored dressing table, everything appeared sterile and as idle as the rest of her home. Above her bed was the only indication that I'd entered the right apartment: a framed poster of Whitney clad in a skimpy leather bikini, elbow-length black gloves and knee-high spiked boots. A muscle-bound man draped in chains was kneeling next to her, one arm wrapped around her thigh, the other hidden behind her buttocks.

Above them in huge block letters was the caption: *Chain-Chain-Chain! Chain of Drools!* Someone named *P. Rick Strong* had been given top billing along with Whitney, and as I got closer to the poster, I searched the list for a supporting cast and eventually located *Jesse Hellion* near the bottom.

I looked into the heavily made-up eyes and blood red lips of Whitney Blue, adult film star, and realized she looked almost nothing like her businesswoman counterpart. On the street, even the most seasoned porn fan probably wouldn't recognize her. I focused briefly on the unicorn tattoo on her breast then continued my search.

The bureau and closet were filled with expensive clothes and a seemingly endless array of shoes but nothing out of the ordinary. I left the bedroom, approached a door that stood closed at the very end of the hall and turned the knob.

Locked.

Squatting, I used my cigarette lighter to get a better look. There was a keyhole on the face of the knob, one of the easiest locks to break. I took a pen from my jacket pocket, removed the cap and carefully inserted the tip of the pocket clip into the lock. I jiggled it, pushed deeper until I felt it catch, then gave a gentle turn. The lock didn't give, but the pen cap did.

I held the lighter closer, saw that the pocket clip had snapped off and was now lodged in the keyhole. "Sonofabitch."

I tried turning the knob just for the hell of it, but the door wouldn't budge. At that point, the only thing I had less of than time was patience. I stood up, braced myself against the wall and gave the door a solid kick. Three tries later the frame splintered and the door slowly swung open.

A strong sulfuric odor similar to a recently lighted match bled into the hallway, and beyond the doorway was darkness so thick I felt compelled to reach out and touch it. When I did, I realized a black silk curtain had been hung from ceiling to floor just inside the entrance. Unable to find any breaks in the fabric, I crawled under it and once on the other side, ignited my lighter.

Through flickering light I saw a small wooden altar positioned near the back wall, an inverted crucifix hanging behind it. A perfect bright-red pentagram had been painted on the floor in front of the altar, and a countless array of black candles lay scattered throughout the windowless room.

With Earl Watson's story of human sacrifice ringing in my ears, I hesitantly approached the altar. An ornate gold chalice sat at the center, two long daggers on either side of it, and a Satanic Bible rested in the upper left-hand corner. Across the front of the altar, 666 had been painted in what appeared to be blood.

In addition to the obvious theatrics of such a setting, I felt an undeniable presence in the room, something deeper and with more meaning than the trinkets and set design straight out of a low-budget horror flick. The sensation of doom, darkness and absolute evil was nearly overwhelming, as if all the horrible events that had taken place here continued to exist, lingering in the air like foul odors.

Once I'd determined that the area behind the altar was empty, I moved on. There were no lights or fixtures of any kind, and my lighter only allowed for a foot or two at best, but I eventually located a closet to the right of the entrance.

The door was unlocked and opened to reveal several hooded red and black silk robes suspended from hangers. I slid them out of the way and brought my lighter around for a closer look.

A fur-covered face with empty eye sockets and long twisted horns emerged from the rear of the closet.

"Christ almighty!" I sprang back, my breath leaving me in one violent rush and the .38 firmly in my grasp even before I'd reached the door.

The face, silent and motionless, hung amidst the silk robes.

A hideous mask. Half human, half goat.

Feeling a bit foolish, I wiped sweat from my forehead with the back of my sleeve, doubled over and drew a series of deep breaths.

The lighter was overheating and had begun to burn my hand so I shut it off and stood in the darkness, telling myself again and again that I needed to calm down and think clearly.

Discovering this room had only served to further confirm what I already knew, and it wasn't going to get me any closer to finding Jesse. I stuffed the .38 in my belt and headed for the exit.

A strong tug ripped the curtain from the doorway, and once it had spiraled to the floor, I stepped over it and crossed the hallway to the only room I'd not yet searched.

The third bedroom had been converted into an office. I rounded a large desk showcasing a computer, dual-line phone, answering machine and fax, and was about to search the drawers when I saw movement from the corner of my eye.

Even before my hand had reached the .38 the room was flooded with bright, clarifying light.

In the doorway stood Kevin Niedermeyer.

Chapter 20

"Niedermeyer?"

"Hello, David." He unbuttoned his suit jacket, loosened his tie. "Whitney and I have been waiting for you in the living room for a few minutes now. Care to join us for a drink?"

My fingers touched steel, pulled the .38 free and held it from view against my thigh. "I don't know what it is, maybe I'm coming down with something, but I'm not feeling very sociable. It's been a *hell* of a week, Kev."

"I'm afraid it'll get worse before it gets better, as they say."

"Think so?"

"Why don't we have that drink now?"

I stood up, showed him the gun and motioned toward the hallway with it. "After you."

He glanced at the weapon and shook his head. "If we wanted to kill you, David, you'd already be dead and buried."

"Wish I could say the same." I leveled the .38 at him and met his gaze. "Move it, asshole."

I followed him out of the office and back down the hallway to the living room, keeping a few feet between us. Just as he'd said, Whitney was standing at the bar mixing drinks.

She looked over at me, smiled and held up a glass, ever the gracious hostess. "Vodka's your poison, isn't it, David?"

"You," I said to Niedermeyer, "sit down."

He looked at Whitney and shrugged. "I tried to explain the gun was unnecessary, but—"

"*Sit.*" Once he'd lowered himself onto the edge of the couch, I returned my attention to Whitney. "I went to see your pal Watson earlier."

She folded her arms across her chest and leaned against the bar. "I thought you might."

"He had a little accident. We were talking when all of a sudden his forehead ran into one of the bullets from this gun."

"You've done even better than we expected," she said.

I moved a bit closer. "Apparently this thing has a nasty habit of going off by itself. Spooky, I know, but it could happen again at any minute, and since I'd hate to see your pretty little face spattered all over the wall, I'm only going to ask this once. Where's Jesse?"

Whitney reached for a notepad on the bar, tore free a single sheet of paper and held it out for me. "Earl followed the bus she took from Worcester to Cape Cod. She got off in Provincetown, rented one of those adorable little cottages down on the beach. I'll bet she got a great price this time of year."

I snatched the paper from her hand, glanced at it long enough to make sure there was an address written on it and stuffed it into my pocket. "Have a seat." She started toward one of the chairs but I stopped her with a wave of the gun. "On the couch with him," I said. "I want you both where I can see you."

She rolled her eyes and did as I'd told her. "Put the gun away and stop being so melodramatic. What are you going to do, fire that thing in the dead of night in the middle of an apartment building full of people?"

"Only twice," I answered. "Unless I get lucky and hit both of you pieces of shit with the same round. Stranger things have happened, just ask the Warren Commission."

Niedermeyer laughed lightly. "It's good to see you've retained your sense of humor, David. You'll need it."

"He's terrified," Whitney said with a smile. "It's written all over his face."

"Mmm," Niedermeyer agreed. "I can smell it."

They were right, of course, but I kept up the tough guy routine anyway. "It's answer time. Niedermeyer, you first."

He arched his eyebrows. "I don't understand."

"No? Maybe this'll help." In one quick motion, I stepped forward, slapped the side of his head with the butt of the .38 and moved back.

Niedermeyer cried out, brought his hands to his head and doubled over. "Jesus Christ!"

"He's not gonna help you, dipshit."

When he sat up, his fingers were slick with blood. A slow trickle leaked from his hairline down the side of his face.

"Hurts like a motherfucker, doesn't it?"

He stared at me, shocked. "Are you insane?"

"Probably." I kept them in my line of sight and slid over to the bar. I knocked aside the drink Whitney had mixed for me, grabbed the bottle and took a pull from that. "I want answers. Now."

While Niedermeyer took a handkerchief from his inside

jacket pocket and held it against the wound, Whitney sat looking at me like a child waiting to open presents on Christmas morning. "I told you he had a violent nature," she said. "He's perfect."

Niedermeyer nodded despite the pain he was obviously in. "I've known Whitney for years," he said. "In fact, she first introduced me to Randy Wallace. Through Randy, I eventually met Jesse."

"That was an impressive act you put on back at your apartment," I told him. "You had me convinced you'd lost a loved one."

"I had."

"You loved Randy?"

"Of course I loved him."

"Then why did you have him killed?"

He looked at me as if the question was too ridiculous to answer. "Randy was always very low-key concerning his involvement in our church. He even kept it hidden from close friends like Jesse. Unfortunately he never viewed our practices too seriously. For him it was more a form of expression, I suppose, a way to be a part of something, a way to belong. Until the night Whitney transformed our beliefs into reality, I think Randy considered our little get-togethers little more than bad theater. But when he realized exactly what he was truly a part of, it terrified him. Since Jesse had no idea that any of us other than Whitney were involved, Randy knew she'd come to us for help. He made me promise we'd do nothing to harm her, and I agreed. He adored Jesse. We gave her a place to hide until you came looking for her, only we overestimated your investigation skills, and by the time you found me she was already gone. Randy knew what was happening. He knew it was your soul Balberith really wanted, not Jesse's, but he also knew that if that didn't happen, he'd settle for the latter, and Randy was afraid you wouldn't find her in time. That meant Jesse was doomed, so he threatened to go against us. I never actually believed he'd do it, but when we heard Abdiel had become involved I knew it was true. At that point we had no choice. Randy had to die. He'd betrayed us and could no longer be trusted." Niedermeyer dabbed at the blood and, realizing it had stopped, tossed the stained handkerchief onto the coffee table. "I loved Randy, David. I didn't want to do it but...as Whitney says, our master must come before all else. *All* else..."

"Okay," I said, "are you even remotely aware that you're out of your fucking minds, or is this like news to you guys?"

"Oh, David, stop it," Whitney snapped. "We know the things going through your mind. We know the things you've been seeing. Do you still doubt their existence?"

"You think just because you performed some sick ritual that—"

"Jesse came to me," she interrupted. "I was her only friend—she had nowhere else to turn. You were on the other side of the world fighting a war, and she was alone, frightened and vulnerable. She had no idea what her future would hold and that terrified her. I showed her the way. I gave her what she wanted, David. It was an opportunity for me to gain a higher level of spiritual power and I took it. All of us, including Jesse, got exactly what we wanted."

"You're a liar."

"That's what she thought until she was staring Balberith

in the eyes and the deal was actually struck. Even then I'm not certain she fully understood the ramifications, but then Lord Satan held up his end of the bargain and sent Balberith to collect was what rightfully his."

"Jesse's soul." Niedermeyer grinned.

"You expect me to believe Jesse sold her soul to the Devil?"

"You already know this is all true," Whitney said. "Once Jesse realized the same, she ran. When Randy betrayed us and Abdiel approached you, we knew you'd try to find her. When you agreed, yet another opportunity presented itself. The chance to deliver a darker soul to our master…"

"Mine," I said. The two of them sat staring at me with those maniacal smiles. "Even if that was possible, why would Jesse do such a thing?"

Whitney crossed her legs, purposely allowing her skirt to ride up her thigh. "Why do you think?"

"What was the deal? Her soul for—"

"Go to her," Niedermeyer said. "Go to her and find out for yourself. It's the only way."

I pointed the .38 at his head. "Answer me."

"You're the only one who can save her, David."

"What was the deal?"

Whitney began to laugh. "Oh, I wish you could've been there. You saw the altar; you felt the power. Imagine Jesse stripped naked and sprawled out across that same altar, dripping with the blood of a sacrificial lamb. Imagine the stupid cunt repeating the words I'd given her, reciting them through tears and pledging her allegiance to Satan while Earl Watson and a dozen others took turns fucking her."

"That's enough."

"Picture her sucking the shit from my ass as we chanted the prayers that made her wish, her sacrifice, reality." Whitney sprung from the chair, eyes wild and her breasts rising and falling with each excited breath. "Imagine Jesse on her knees like an obedient little whore, praising our master's name."

I'd become so focused on Whitney I didn't see Niedermeyer rush me until it was too late.

He hit me in the midsection with his shoulder and sent both of us flying. We landed near the bar, him on top of me, his hands clenched around my throat.

The impact of the collision knocked the .38 from my hand, and although I could see it on the floor just inches from us, it was beyond my reach. Niedermeyer's hands were surprisingly powerful, and as his grip tightened my vision started to blur. I put both hands under his chin and pushed up, forcing his head back until he was faced with either loosening his hold or having his neck snapped. He chose the former, and as he did, I lifted my knee up into his crotch.

Niedermeyer gagged and fell off me, and as I fought to regain my breath I saw Whitney pounce on the gun and dash back over to the couch.

Before I could get to my feet Niedermeyer was on me again, this time grabbing me from behind. His hands locked onto my throat and the room tilted and began to spin as his fingers severed the oxygen to my brain.

I reached around, took his head in my hands and leaned into him until my back was braced against his chest. Pulling down, I crushed his throat into my shoulder and saw Whitney watching us with the same aroused look.

"Do it!" she screamed at me. "Do it!"

Locking my fingers in his hair, I gave a single violent yank, snapped his head down over my shoulder and broke his neck.

I released him and he collapsed to the floor like a rag doll, vacant eyes open.

A gush of dark blood spilled from his mouth, and as Niedermeyer exhaled his last gurgling breath, I struggled to my feet and looked over at Whitney. Standing by the window with the .38 in hand, she nodded rapidly and again began to laugh.

I swallowed, coughed and massaged my aching throat while still trying to catch my breath. "You better kill me, because if I get that away from you I'm gonna empty it between your eyes."

"I'd rather have it between my legs," she said with a smile, running the barrel along the side of her breast. "You and I are going to make a hell of a team, David...literally."

"Fuck you."

"There'll be plenty of time for that." She brought the gun to her lips and traced the cylinder with her tongue. "Don't fight it. Accept it. Worship it. Deep down, you know it's where you belong, where you were born to be."

"You're wrong."

Whitney's eyes widened. "Welcome home, David."

Before I could reach her, she dropped the gun, threw her arms into the air and vaulted backwards through the window.

As she disappeared into the night, shards of jagged glass rained down across the floor and an icy wind blew puffs of snow through the newly formed portal.

I stood motionless for what seemed an eternity as the shock of what she'd done slowly took hold. Then I ran to what was left of the window, ripped the remaining curtains out of the way and looked down at the street two stories below.

Whitney had landed on her back just beyond a parked car. Her shattered body lay twisted in the snow, a halo of blood quickly soaking the blanket of white surrounding her.

I knelt down, grabbed the .38 and slipped it into my coat pocket while Niedermeyer's dead eyes stared up at me from the floor.

Sounds of sudden activity from the apartment below snapped my dazed mind back into focus. I hurried through the living room to the kitchen and headed for the fire escape.

By the time I reached the corner at the top of the block, a small crowd of people had gathered around Whitney's body, and approaching sirens could be heard in the distance.

I pulled the crumpled paper she'd given me from my pocket and read the address in Provincetown scribbled across it.

"Jesse," I whispered, "I'm on my way."

Chapter 21

Fighting sleep, I grabbed Route 3 just outside the city, followed it all the way to the Sagamore Bridge and crossed over onto 6A, the highway to Provincetown. Situated at the very tip of Cape Cod, my destination was still nearly an hour away. The snow had let up some along the coast but harsh winds brandished the powder about in swirling clouds, making actual accumulation difficult to estimate and driving along the lonely highway far more adventurous than it should have been.

I cracked the window and lit a cigarette. Tiny spikes of icy snow tickled my cheek but the fresh air felt good against my warm skin. The vision of Whitney's shattered body continued to haunt me, slipping past my mind's eye like headlights from a passing car creeping along the walls of a darkened room. As quickly as her memory faded, the gut-wrenching crack of Kevin Niedermeyer's neck seeped to the forefront, his wide lifeless eyes gawking at me from the deepest recesses of my brain.

I found myself sobbing like a child. There had been so much violence, so much bloodshed. Why did death follow me like a storm cloud? Maybe Whitney had spoken the truth.

Welcome home, David.

* * *

I didn't realize my eyes had slid shut until I opened them in mid-scream.

Someone was in the road, but I'd had no idea they were there until I saw a blur of movement separate from the snow. A horrifying thud followed and the body flew up over the hood and crashed into the windshield.

Slamming the brake, I felt the back end of the car fishtail. I cut the wheel and held the brake until the violent spin ended. The sudden stop caused the car to jerk forward then back. The body, still a vague shadow, was launched back into the night.

I sat staring into the darkness, following the headlights and trying to see anything beyond the beams and the endless swirling flakes of snow. My grip on the steering wheel was so strong my palms ached. I released the wheel, listened to the pounding of my heart and the rapid cadence of my breath.

The idea that someone would've been walking in the middle of 6A in the midst of a snowstorm seemed unlikely at best, but then again, this sort of blowing snow was disorienting, particularly when on foot. If the person had broken down and attempted to walk to the next exit, they easily could have lost their bearings and ended up in the center of the two-lane highway.

The windshield wipers squeaked back and forth, droned on with the purr of the car heater. I wiped perspiration from my forehead, pushed open the door and forced myself into the storm.

I left the door open so the interior light could provide greater visibility and the normally annoying reminder chime could act as an audible homing device were I to lose visual contact with the car.

The windshield hadn't sustained any damage I could see, so I moved around to the front of the car, steadying myself against it. Icy particles stabbed at my eyes and peppered my face but I pushed on and looked out at the small section of road illuminated by the headlights. There was nothing in the road or to the sides, no sign of a body, only snow and darkness. I trudged along a bit further, but still, nothing.

"Hello!" My voice sounded foreign and muffled in the wind. I turned and started back toward the car.

A dog that resembled a Doberman, but that was considerably larger than any such breed I had ever seen, sat idly next to the driver's side door, watching me. I stopped, squinted through the storm at it. Twin fire-red orbs stared back and a low growl cut the night.

This was not a dog of this Earth.

I heard distant whining and barking noises as more eyes emerged from the twists of snow and settled behind the lead dog. There were at least five or six of them. I could hear their fervent breathing even above the wind. Although I was freezing, I stood perfectly still. If I reached for the .38, I knew I wouldn't get to it in time, and running was pointless, but the growling grew louder and the dogs shuffled about, teeth bared, pointed ears drawn back.

Since I was facing the front of the car, I knew the median strip followed by two more lanes of highway were to my right. To my left was a breakdown lane, then forest. I stole a glance in that direction but couldn't gauge distances in this weather.

I flexed my fingers, already stiff and growing numb in the cold, and worked them slowly until I felt the blood returning, then turned and sprinted toward the woods.

My feet slipped and slid but I pushed harder, running fast as I could toward the side of the road, curtains of snow blinding me as I went. The beasts followed—I could hear them barking now—their jaws snapping at my heels.

I launched myself from the edge of the breakdown lane toward the woods, rolled through the fall and scrambled back to my feet.

But they were already on me, tugging at my arms, taking my legs out from under me, teeth tearing and yanking, pulling me down to the ground, ripping me to pieces. Flashes of white fangs, flying drool, wild eyes and clawed paws exploded through sounds of flesh being torn from bone, bone being cracked, and my tortured, gurgling screams of agony.

I felt something slam violently against my face—like I'd been punched—as one of the creatures bit into my cheek and jerked loose a slab of meat. Rolling, I tried to shield my eyes as searing pain exploded through me, the sticky warm spray of blood mixing with the ironically beautiful flakes of snow.

"David, you're safe, baby, you're safe."

I opened my eyes, struggled to focus on my surroundings: a small, unfamiliar room, sparse moonlight leaking through the only window on the far wall. Soft hands caressed my neck, back and shoulders and I turned toward them, ignoring the pain still coursing through my body.

"Jess?" Her name felt strange as it formed on my lips,

as if I hadn't spoken it in a very long time.

Sitting next to me on the edge of the bed, she pushed a wisp of hair from my face and smiled. "Were you expecting someone else?"

"*Jess*," I said, emotion catching in my throat. Her skin smelled vaguely of talcum powder. "There were dogs…they…they were—"

"It's all right," she said dreamily, her fingers stroking my hair. "They're gone now."

I reached up, touched her face with my hand, noticed an array of puncture wounds and dried blood along my arm and disfigured hand. "Get me to a hospital."

"It's okay," she whispered. "I'm going to take care of you, baby."

I felt too weak to sit up, but my eyes followed her hands as they retrieved a small washbasin from the floor next to the bed. Resting it on her knees, she reached inside with both hands, removed a sponge and wrung it out. She ran it against my forehead, and the warm water felt nice. "I was trying to find you," I said, "but you found me."

Jesse finished my sponge bath without speaking, then set the washbasin aside and stood up. My eyes closed. When they opened, she was over me again, this time covering me with a drab-looking blanket.

"Where are we?" I asked.

She offered a sly smile. "Where would you like to be?"

"Home," I said, my voice cracking. "I want to be home with you, just the two of us, like it used to be."

Her hand touched my face, lingered on my cheek as if feeling it for the first time. "Shhh." She offered an almost drowsy frown and knelt down next to the bed. As she leaned closer, I felt her lips brush mine. Her tongue, hot and moist, gently licked my wounds.

She moved lower. Behind her sat the dog, watching silently from the shadowy corner of the room.

Tears welled in my eyes. "Jess…Christ…*Jess*…"

"It's okay, baby." She pulled back. Blood stained her lips. "It's okay."

She got to her feet and padded to the corner. Eyes still watching me, she opened the door and the dog strode from the room.

My vision still blurred, I blinked the tears from my eyes, felt them roll along my cheeks.

Jesse closed the door, her back to me now. "I've missed you, baby," she said.

Without turning around she pulled her shirt off over her head, dropped it to the floor, then peeled down her jeans and stepped out of them. Looking over her shoulder at me, she offered the same whimsical smile she had before then hitched her thumbs in her panties and pulled them down, bending forward and pushing her backside toward me as she did so.

My eyes followed the curve of her lower back to the rounded halves of her ass…and the several feet of scale-covered tail slithering about at the base of her spine.

"Help me," I whispered. "God in Heaven, *help me*."

The voices in my head led me back, away from the hallucinations, trickery and terror, until only uncertainty and denial remained. Lingering beneath a guillotine poised to strike, lost in a labyrinth with no beginning or end, I realized I knew nothing at all. Fantasy, reality, good and evil had merged, festering within me like a cancer butchering everything in its path.

The car was pulled to the side of a dark, desolate road. Through snowflakes dancing in the headlight beams, I saw a sign fastened to a wooden post and a large sand dune beyond.

Cabins by the Sea—Vacancy.

Hands trembling and moist with sweat, I reached for the paper, verified the address and cabin number then tossed it into the back seat. On the far side of the dune, several cottages were scattered along a ridge overlooking the ocean. All were dark.

Except one.

Pelted by snow, I leaned into a violent wind whipping in off the Atlantic and trudged up the steep slope of the sand dune. At the summit, I pulled off Earl Watson's trench coat, threw it into the darkness and zipped closed my leather jacket. A yellow light struggling through the whirling snow provided just enough illumination to expose a path down the slanted dune. Squinting, I recognized the source of the beacon peeking out a thinly curtained window from the cottage below, and started towards it.

I slipped near the base, felt my ankle turn and tumbled to the ground with a muffled grunt. Burning pain shot all the way up to my knee. I leaned forward, plunged my hands beneath more than an inch of freezing slush and pushed myself up into a sitting position. Despite a throbbing ache pulsing through my ankle, I freed the leg pinned beneath me and managed to regain my feet.

Limping now, and wincing with each step, I tucked chin against chest and closed on the cottage, stopping a few feet from the front door. Cheeks frozen, eyes watering, I raised my head. The cottage was tiny, probably no more than one main room and a full bath. Three wooden steps and a narrow front porch were all that separated me from life, death, deliverance or damnation, yet none of that mattered anymore. All I wanted—all I prayed for—was closure.

Whatever my destiny, it would be decided here, on this night, in this place.

Chapter 22

I climbed the steps, a howling wind and the steady roar of waves crashing the nearby beach distracting me from the pain hammering in my ankle. Unsure of who or what I might find, I kept one hand on the .38, leaned against a section of wall alongside the front door and peeked through one of the windows.

Through the flimsy curtain I scanned the main room. A bed against the far wall was still made, and clothes and other personal items were strewn across the floor from an open suitcase at the foot. The shade from a lamp on the nightstand had been removed and tossed aside, the bare bulb filling the cottage with harsh light. There was a cheap veneer bureau, a wicker rocking chair, several framed paintings of typical rustic settings—reproductions of the Atlantic Coast, lighthouses and such—and a large throw rug which covered most of the floor just beyond the entrance.

There was no sign of a telephone or television, but from my position I could see a tiny gas stove, sink and icebox all located in one small area, and an adjacent bathroom veiled in darkness.

I reached for the door, turned the knob and felt it open without resistance. Surprised but undeterred I slipped inside, the .38 leading the way.

I was greeted by a burst of dry heat, and as I closed the door behind me the clamor of the storm softened. I hesitated, allowing my eyes and ears to adjust to the interior of the cottage.

The clothes in the suitcase and on the bed belonged to a woman, as did the sneakers, socks, jeans, sweater and blouse that formed a trail along the floor to the bathroom. On the nightstand was a half-empty bottle of vodka and a Bible draped in rosary beads. The kitchen area had been littered with an assortment of candy wrappers, spent cola cans and discarded bags from a fast-food restaurant. A cigarette was doing a slow burn in an ashtray on the bureau, a crumpled pack and disposable lighter next to it. I recognized the brand as the same Jesse had smoked the last time I'd seen her, and turned my attention to the partially open bathroom door.

Stepping over the last article of clothing, I leaned against the outer door frame and listened. Although muffled by the wind, the steady cadence of heavy breathing was unmistakable. I clutched the .38 with both hands and hit the door with my shoulder, wheeling around into a shooting stance as it swung open.

Beyond the sight of the gun was a sink with a mirror above it, a toilet and a stall shower. Jesse was sitting on the floor clad in panties and a bra, legs stretched out in front of her and a slender length of rubber tubing fastened just above her left elbow. A syringe, used pack of matches and a small blackened spoon had been left on the lip of the sink, and the acrid stench of recently cooked heroin still hung in the air.

Her head bobbed forward then back, as if she'd lost all control of her neck, and through glazed eyes she looked at me, apparently unaware of my presence until that exact moment.

I lowered the gun and watched her. I'd been certain that once I'd finally found her, I'd know exactly what to say and how to say it, but now the words refused to come.

Jesse's hair was still bleached, but she'd hacked most of it off—with pruning shears from the look—and her face was pale, heavily lined for someone so young. She'd lost a considerable amount of weight and her once beautiful emerald eyes, saddled with dark circles, had turned distant and dull.

"Jess…"

She squinted, not yet recognizing me. "Who…who's there…"

I jammed the .38 in my belt and approached her hesitantly. She had a long history of occasional drug use but I'd never known her to use heroin, and after all I'd been through I wanted to be sure it was really Jesse I was dealing with.

"Jess," I said again, squatting next to her. "It's me."

Her eyes widened and her chapped lips moved but made no sound. Slowly, as recognition dawned across her face she grimaced and began to weep. "David…oh, David—*no*."

"It's all right." I removed the tube from her arm and threw it aside. "I'm here now."

I reached for her hands but she leaned back against the wall as if hoping to dissolve through it. "No—no, don't. You've got to go—please just—just go."

"Everything's going to be all right."

"How did you find me?"

I reached for her again. "I've got to get you out of

here." My hands touched cold shoulders and her body went rigid and tense. "How much of this crap did you take?"

"Not enough." She pawed at the tears trickling down her cheeks. "It's not the running that's so bad...I've been running all my life, right? It's the—the waiting. The shit doesn't make it any easier...just makes it so I don't care. You've got to go, David. Why—why did you come here? That's what they want—don't you know that's what they want?"

I grabbed her under each arm and lifted her to her feet, steadying myself as she flopped against me, her full weight igniting the pain in my ankle. "We have to get out of here."

"It won't matter," she whispered. "It won't matter."

Once we'd reached the main room, I sat her down on the edge of the bed. Her crying had become more violent and her eyes were darting from one end of the cottage to the other. "Listen to me. Jess, *listen* to me." I took her face in both hands and turned it toward me. "They're all dead, do you understand? Whitney Blue, Kevin Niedermeyer, Randy Wallace, Walter Rizzi, Earl Watson, all of them dead."

She gave a groggy, woeful smile. "It doesn't matter."

"Tell me what happened."

"I loved you." Her hands found my waist. "That's what happened."

"Jess—"

"And they punished me for it," she sobbed. "Now they want to punish you."

"Why didn't you come to me for help?"

"I didn't want you to find me, I—" She looked at me,

lips trembling. "You have to go, David. Please, you have to go."

I began to gather her clothes from the floor. "You're coming with me."

She shook her head. "I can't."

"It's not open to discussion. Come on, let's get you dressed."

"You don't understand," she snapped, struggling to her feet. "After everything that's happened, you still don't understand."

"Then explain it to me."

Her expression shifted from fear to anger and she wobbled on unsteady feet. "Just get out—go! Get out!"

I placed her clothes on the bed. "I'll carry you kicking and screaming if I have to."

She collapsed back onto the bed, her head in her hands. "The deal was made years ago. Nothing can stop it now."

I remembered the vodka on the nightstand, limped over to the bottle and took a long pull. Watching her there on the bed—the swell of her breasts barely contained in a delicate bra, a hint of brown hair visible through the thin panties, her soft legs covered in goose pimples and bare toes stroking the coarse rug—nothing seemed capable of diminishing her beauty. Not the pain, terror and exhaustion etched across her face, not the red eyes swollen with tears, not even the marks left by needles in the bend of her arm or my knowledge of her past, present and probable future. Window dressing and inconsequential diversion aside, all I felt for her in that surreal instant was unconditional love.

"Jesse," I asked, the vodka warming my throat and

beyond, "what was the deal?"

Her eyes locked on mine and somewhere deep within them I saw a glimmer of who she had once been. "You always loved me, David, but you never had faith in me, never believed in me. When you beat that man to death and they threw you off the police force, you could've turned to me—should've turned to me—but you didn't. I could've taken care of you if only you'd let me. We could've stayed together, gotten through anything—you didn't have to run. You didn't have to go off to that goddamn desert and fight somebody else's war."

I put the bottle aside. "We wanted different things."

"No, we didn't. We just had different ideas about how to get them." She moved closer, walking carefully on still shaky legs. "You didn't want me to be an actress. You didn't want me to have the fame and fortune I'd dreamed about since I was a little girl, you didn't—"

"That's not true. It was a matter of priorities, Jess. *This* is what I didn't want for you."

"What you never understood was that I would have given all of it up for you," she said softly. "And eventually did."

Her words hit me like a runaway train. "Jess…Jesus Christ…what did you do?"

She hugged herself. "I gave them my soul."

I felt my eyes grow moist. "For what?"

No reply.

"For what!"

"For you."

I braced myself against the nightstand. "No."

"To bring you home safely." Her face blurred through my tears. "I didn't want you to die."

I walked past her, sat on the edge of the bed and began to remember. The wind shook the cottage, its howl our only companion until my thoughts became words. "When you think about the desert, you think of unbearable heat. But at night it turns cold." I forced myself to look at her. "Recently murdered bodies throw off a surprising amount of heat—did you know that? Enough to get you through the night so long as you don't mind blanketing yourself in corpses."

"David—"

"Do you honestly think I could go through something like that and ever be the same?" I stood up, put my arms around her. "I was meant to die in that desert, Jess…it never seemed real that even with my training I could've killed them all without even one of them waking up that night. That's because it wasn't real, was it? I was supposed to die that night, not them. Most days, I wish I had."

"But I saved you," she said helplessly. "Don't you see?" Jesse put her head against my chest. "It's too late now. We can't stop it."

"We'll run."

"No. It's over."

"*She's right, you know.*"

I spun in the direction of the voice, pushed Jesse out of the way onto the bed and drew the .38 from my belt.

Balberith stood just inside the entrance grinning at me. "I let myself in, hope you don't mind. It's colder than Martha Stewart out there."

I fired twice, hitting his shoulder with the first round and the center of his chest with the second. The impact sent him staggering back but didn't drop him. I stepped closer and emptied the gun, shooting him in the thigh, abdomen and forehead.

With an entry wound clearly visible between his eyes Balberith regained his balance and gazed at the collection of holes in his clothes. "For Christ's sake." He sighed. "You've ruined a perfectly marvelous suit."

The gun fell from my hand, bounced across the floor. I could hear Jesse whimpering behind me but couldn't take my eyes from Balberith's hideous features.

"You know why I'm here," he said. "Get out of the way."

"Eat shit."

He slowly closed the gap between us. "Don't worry your demented little head about it. I'll take good care of her. She'll be right at home with her ass in the air in Hell."

I charged him but he grabbed my throat, his clawed hand lifting me from the floor and holding me there effortlessly. I tried to kick him, missed, and he tightened his grip, shaking me with such force I feared he might snap my spine. As spit bubbled from my mouth and my body went limp, he released me, dropping me back to my feet, and with one short thrust, sent me sprawling across the room.

Crashing against the far wall, I slid back to the floor. As my head cleared, I scrambled to my feet and rushed him again. He rolled his eyes, backhanded me, and I found myself returned to midair.

I landed on the nightstand, knocking it and the lamp to the floor. Rolling away from the broken pieces, I remained on all fours, ignored the pain and tried to catch my breath. I grabbed the edge of the bed and pulled myself up, my legs aching and unstable.

"Stay down, David."

"Fuck you." I hobbled toward him. "You're gonna have to kill me."

Balberith smoothed the few hairs on the top of his bald dome then just as casually straightened his silk tie. "Are you aware that there's a very fine line between bravery and stupidity? You shot me with five bullets and I complained about my suit. Now you want to have a fist fight? Don't be an ass."

"David," I heard Jesse sob, "stop."

Without looking back at her, I dropped my arms to my side and gave Balberith the submissive nod he wanted.

"All right." He smiled. "Now that you've gotten that out of your system let's get down to business, shall we? Jesse and I have an appointment and it's time to go. Of course you're welcome to join us if you'd like."

Before I could respond, Balberith was distracted. He looked past me, bared his fangs and hissed, spitting like a frightened cat.

I turned and saw Abdiel sitting in the wicker rocking chair, as relaxed as if he'd been there all along.

"You know the rules," he said to Balberith. "You can't have them both."

"I'm here to collect what's rightfully mine," he growled. "This has nothing to do with you."

Abdiel shrugged. "You know the rules."

"I never liked you," Balberith said, relaxing a bit as he turned back to me. "Even in the old days when we were all on the same side—couldn't stand the bastard."

"Be quiet." Abdiel rose from the chair and stood between us, clearly relishing the fear his presence had summoned in his enemy. For the first time, I saw in him the confidence of an ancient warrior, a sword in God's army just as legend had described. "Fools should do their best never to speak."

"I only want what's mine."

"You're an errand boy."

Balberith smiled. "So are you."

"You never were too bright."

"Mind your own business. Isn't there a harp somewhere that needs strumming?"

"Don't make me angry, little worm."

"Fine." The demon backed away. "Say your piece then get out of my way."

Abdiel faced me. "Jesse made her own decisions, David. She exercised free will. Not even God Himself will interfere with that, do you understand?"

"Please—"

"There's nothing I can do," he said flatly. "I'm sorry."

I looked to Balberith's black eyes. "It's me you want," I reminded him.

He licked his lips and nodded.

Abdiel put a hand on my shoulder. "You also have free will," he told me. "But if you make this decision there will be no turning back."

"No!" Jesse screamed, fell from the bed and crawled across the floor. Crying, she reached up for me. "Don't—don't you do that. Don't you do that...for *me*."

I took her hands in mine and kissed them, tasting our tears as they streamed into my mouth. "I love you."

She stared at me, her chin trembling so violently she was unable to speak, her grip on me so powerful it had become painful.

I looked to Abdiel. "She'll be safe?"

He nodded. "She'll be free."

"Forever?"

"For as long as she chooses to be."

"And me?"

With an expression both joyless and sympathetic, Abdiel shook his head in the negative.

I leaned over, kissed Jesse's cheek and wiped the tears from her eyes. Through the window behind her, the vista had softened. Night had become early morning, and though darkness remained, it was slowly dying, giving way to the light faintly reflected off blankets of freshly fallen snow.

Gently, I stroked Jesse's hair, looked again at Abdiel, and then at Balberith.

"Take me."

1991

Chapter 23

The idea that I might be an alcoholic had never crossed my mind in any serious context because I'd always had access to liquor. Once cut off from it, however, the concept struck me not only as possible, but likely. My symptoms were subtle. No vomiting, violent shakes or sweating spells, rather an odd sensation of sluggish detachment from daily life and a series of stressful aches and pains that were dimly uncomfortable if not outright painful. For me, withdrawal was more psychological than physical— quiet thoughts, uncertainty, and like a mathematician calculating countless formulas in search of solutions, a state where each scenario, fear and possibility was considered and dissected from every conceivable angle over and over again.

"How are you feeling today?" my doctor would ask at each visit.

"Fine," I'd reply.

"Are you sure?" he'd ask.

"Does it matter?"

"Of course," he'd say, frowning. "You look like you're in pain."

"I am in pain."

"Would you like to talk about it?"

"Not particularly."

"I can't stress how important it is to discuss your feelings," he'd insist. "It's going to take time, and we'll both have to exercise patience. Things aren't going to turn around unless we work through these issues. Your alcoholism only complicates the psychological issues we're dealing with here, do you understand? Silence perpetuates the problems and allows them to fester. Medication can only do so much. True healing begins with acknowledgment, confrontation and honest evaluation. Eventual resolution can be achieved—I promise you—but it's a process, David, an ongoing process."

"Right," I'd say. "An ongoing process."

From there, I'd light a cigarette. He'd throw a few more questions my way and I'd ignore them like all the others. By the time my cigarette had burned to the filter he was usually gone, promising to return the next day for more "healing," as if this were something I should be happy about and as if I didn't know what he was really up to.

Time moved so slowly it often seemed like it had come to a standstill, frozen at the precise second I'd realized where I was and the manner in which the remainder of my life would be passed.

Varied degrees of "healing" were required here, depending upon the patient and section of the hospital they'd been assigned to. Those housed in my wing had only minor physical ailments, if any—unlike the poor bastards on the floor below—and were challenged by broken minds and battered wills rather than severed limbs and ravaged bodies. Some of us were drug addicts, others alcoholics, but we all shared two distinct symptoms: combat experience and mental illness. At least that's what they told us.

A voice intruded on my thoughts.

"David, can you hear me?"

The room gradually came into focus to reveal institutional versions of a bed, desk and two chairs surrounded by pristine white walls.

"David? Sweetie?"

My eyes shifted to Jesse. Sitting in a chair across from me, legs crossed and hands folded in her lap, she cocked her head to the side. "Sweetie, can you hear me?"

"Of course I can hear you," I said. "I don't care how crazy I am, it doesn't make me deaf."

She forced a smile. "You weren't answering me."

I looked down at the slippers protruding from the cuffs of my flannel pajamas and vaguely remembered they'd been a gift from her. "Sorry."

"Don't be sorry. How are you feeling?"

I searched my robe for cigarettes but the pockets were empty. "Can I bum a smoke?"

Jesse pulled her purse from the back of her chair and rummaged through it until she'd found a pack of cigarettes. I watched her remove one, light it and then carefully place it between my fingers. "You look a lot better than you did last week," she said with a smile. "How are the sessions with Doctor Rothman going?"

I took a drag on the cigarette, exhaled. "Menthol," I said, studying it. "I don't like menthol."

"I'll bring you a carton of your own next time," she promised. "I was talking with Doctor Rothman a few minutes ago and—"

I handed the cigarette back to her. "They make me cough."

Jesse took it and nodded patiently. "Sweetheart, I was talking with Doctor Rothman a few minutes ago and he said he had some concerns. He said you weren't cooperating the way he'd like and—"

"That's probably true, yeah."

"He's here to help you."

"Yeah, okay."

Jesse leaned forward and lowered her voice. "Don't put so much pressure on yourself, okay? You haven't been back long and Doctor Rothman said things are going to take time. If you'll just trust him, David, you'll be out of here sooner than you think."

I stared at her, wanting to say something but unable to convert my thoughts into words.

"Did you hear what I just said?"

"Yeah, I heard you. Jesus."

She drew a deep breath and sat back. "I wonder."

I wrapped my robe around me and cinched the belt. "They're not like us, you know. The doctors, the nurses, the orderlies. They're...they're not like us."

"How do you mean, sweetie?"

"They're just different, that's all. They try to hide it but...but I've seen them. You have to look at them from the back. That's how you can tell. They got something back there we don't. They try to cover it with their clothes, but sometimes...sometimes you can see it moving." I looked up—the senior nurse stood in the doorway, staring at me.

Devils have tails, Jess.

Struggling against tears now, Jesse followed my gaze and looked over her shoulder. The nurse immediately offered a warm smile and moved away. "You just need to take things one day at a time," she said, turning back to me, trembling. "You need to—"

"Right," I interrupted. "So, what have you been up to?"

Jesse pretended to smile again. "I think you'll be very proud of me. I just signed on with a drama coach in Boston. It's nothing huge, just workshops for now, but it's a start. By the time you're ready to come home, we can start talking about moving. We could both use a change of scenery. Wouldn't it be nice to go somewhere else and just start all over again? New York or maybe Los Angeles would be—"

"Would you do me a favor?" I asked.

"If I can, sure I will."

"I don't want you to come here anymore."

Her awkward discomfort turned to shock. "What are you talking about?"

"I want you to stop visiting me."

Jesse shook her head. "You don't mean that."

"Yes, I do." I slid my chair closer, put a hand on her knee. "You need to get on with your life, Jess."

"You are my life."

"Not anymore." I tightened my grip on her leg. "I love you—you know that—but we both know I'm never coming out of this place."

"That's not true," she said, taking my hands in her own. "You have to give yourself some time. I know you're confused and frightened but you only just got here a few weeks ago, David. Doctor Rothman assures me your problems can be worked out. You've been through hell but you've got to remember that he's dealt with hundreds of others who have been through the same sort of trauma."

I looked into her eyes. "Did you say a few *weeks*?"

"You've been home less than a month."

"How...How could that be?"

"It's okay," she said, kissing my hands. "Everything's going to be fine, you'll see. Doctor Rothman says you have to—"

"Doctor Rothman's a liar and an evil motherfucker." I returned her hands to her lap. "I don't want you to waste your life waiting around for me. I couldn't take becoming a burden to you."

"David, you're not a—"

"Please don't do that to me," I said. "*Please*, Jess."

Jesse straightened her hair and nervously wiped away a tear, smudging eyeliner across her cheek. "Maybe if I gave you a little time, that'd be best. Maybe if I didn't visit for a week or so, you'd—"

"Yes," I agreed, gently wiping the black smear from her face. "No visits for a week or so."

She stood up, slung her purse over her shoulder. "All right," she said softly. "If that's what you want."

"You'll do fine," I told her. "The longer you stay away, the easier it'll become."

Jesse leaned over and kissed me, lightly at first, then passionately. "I'll see you soon, baby."

I nodded, watched her turn and leave the room.

When I was certain she was no longer on the floor, I ventured out into the hallway and moved past the nurses' station where they all stood huddled over reports and medications. Cold stares followed me. I lowered my eyes and continued down the hallway to the recreation room. Several patients were scattered about, some watching television, others playing Ping-Pong or huddled around tables playing cards.

I shuffled over to the window, looked down at the parking lot and what appeared to be a beautiful afternoon. Another patient, a man I'd become friendly with who had been there since Vietnam, wandered away from a conversation he'd been having with someone else and sidled up next to me.

"How's it going, Drago?"

"Hey, Harold," I said without looking at him.

"That chick your girlfriend, brother-man?"

Just then I saw Jesse emerge from the door below and cross the parking lot toward her car. "Huh?"

"The hot little number with the nice tits, the one that just left," he said, craning his neck so he could watch her too. "That your girl?"

I looked down at the crucifix dangling from a chain around my neck, wondered why it was upside down instead of the way I'd always worn it. "She used to be."

"Really?" He grinned lasciviously and rubbed his crotch. "Well. I'll be damned."

"Yeah," I said with a wry smile. "Me too."

ACKNOWLEDGMENTS

Big thanks to Eric Campbell and everyone at Down & Out Books for making this new edition possible. Thanks also to Ray Hoy of The Fiction Works, who, back in the day, believed in this novella when few did. Special thanks to private investigator Mark Hayward for lending his knowledge and invaluable expertise to the research aspects of this project back when it was originally written, and for his gracious cooperation and patience with my seemingly endless questions. Thanks also to my publicist Erin Sweet-Al Mehairi, and to my wife Carol and all my friends and family. And finally, thanks to all my readers and fans across the globe for your continued support.

GREG F. GIFUNE is a professional, internationally-published author of several acclaimed novels, novellas and two short story collections. He resides in Massachusetts with his wife, a few cats and two dogs.

He can be reached online at gfgauthor@verizon.net or on Facebook and Twitter. Visit his official site for updates and info at https://gregfgifune.wordpress.com/.

On the following pages are a few
more great titles from the
Down & Out Books publishing family.

For a complete list of books and to
sign up for our newsletter,
go to DownAndOutBooks.com.

Night Work
Greg F. Gifune

Down & Out Books
978-1-948235-32-7

In the secret worlds of organized crime and the independent professional wrestling circuit of the 1990s, no one is immune to the con, the violence, the hunger for power and respect, the lust and the darkness.

How far would you go for money and supremacy? Who would you betray? What could you tolerate? How much would you sacrifice?

Frank Ponte is about to find out...

Saying Uncle
Greg F. Gifune

Down & Out Books
978-1-946502-90-2

Andy DeMarco and his little sister Angela worship their Uncle Paulie, an enigmatic savior who took the place of their absent father. But one summer day something unspeakable happens to Angela and the world changes forever.

Twenty years later, Andy returns home to bury his murdered uncle, and only now can he begin to understand who the man truly was.

Dangerous Boys
Greg F. Gifune

Down & Out Books
978-1-946502-52-0

All they had was each other…and nothing to lose…

Part coming-of-age tale, part dark crime thriller, *Dangerous Boys* is the story of a group of young punks with nothing left to lose, fighting to find themselves, their futures, and a way out of the madness and darkness before it's too late.

The Unrepentant
E.A. Aymar

Down & Out Books
March 2019
978-1-948235-58-7

Eighteen-year old Charlotte Reyes ran away from an abusive home only to end up tricked, kidnapped, and taken across the country by criminals. Charlotte manages to escape with the help of a reluctant former soldier named Mace Peterson, but she can't seem to shake the gang.

With nowhere to run and nowhere to hide, Charlotte realizes she only has one option.

She has to fight.

The Hurt Business
Stories by Mike Miner

All Due Respect, an imprint of
Down & Out Books
March 2019
978-1-948235-75-4

"We are such fragile creatures."

The men, women and children in these stories will all be pushed to the breaking point, some beyond. Heroes, villains and victims. The lives Miner examines are haunted by pain and violence. They are all trying to find redemption. A few will succeed, but at a terrible price. All of them will face the consequences of their bad decisions as pipers are paid and chickens come home to roost. The lessons in these pages are learned the very hard way. Throughout, Miner captures the savage beauty of these dark tales with spare poetic prose.

The Science of Paul
A **Paul** Little Novel of Crime
Aaron Philip Clark

Shotgun Honey, an imprint of
Down & Out Books
978-1-948235-00-6

Ex-convict Paul Little dreams of starting a new life on a farm in North Carolina but when he gets involved with a petty thug who is later murdered, Paul is pinned between the volatile gangster accused of the crime and the straight-laced detective who sent Paul to prison years ago.

Facing danger at every turn, Paul will have to navigate Philadelphia's mean streets and match his wits with hustlers, cops, and killers.